BEARS
Their Life and Behavior

Other Books by Art Wolfe
Indian Baskets of the Northwest Coast, 1978
The Imagery of Art Wolfe, 1984
Alakshak, The Great Country, 1989
The Kingdom, 1990
Owls: Their Life and Behavior, 1990
Chameleons, Dragons in the Trees, 1991
Light on the Land, 1991
The Art of Nature Photography, 1993
Penguins, Puffins, and Auks, 1993

Other Books by William Ashworth
Hells Canyon: The Deepest Gorge on Earth
The Wallowas: Coming of Age in the Wilderness
The Carson Factor
Under the Influence: Congress, Lobbies, and
        the American Pork Barrel System
Nor Any Drop to Drink
The Late, Great Lakes

Preceding page: A brown bear cub-of-the-year peers from the grass at McNeil River Bear Sanctuary, Alaska.

A brown bear beneath peaks of the Aleutian Range at McNeil River Bear Sanctuary, Alaska.

Overleaf: A brown bear gapes at the camera.

A PHOTOGRAPHIC STUDY OF THE NORTH AMERICAN SPECIES

BEARS
Their Life and Behavior

PHOTOGRAPHS BY ART WOLFE

Text by William Ashworth

Crown Publishers, Inc., New York

Brown bear sow with
two second-year cubs.
Mikfik Creek, Alaska.

Published by Crown Publishers, Inc., 201 East 50th
Street, New York, New York 10022. Member of the
Crown Publishing Group.

CROWN is a trademark of Crown Publishers, Inc.

Manufactured in Japan

Design by Lauren Dong

Library of Congress Cataloging-in-Publication Data
Wolfe, Art.
    Bears, their life and behavior : a photographic
study of the North American species / photographs
by Art Wolfe ; text by William Ashworth.
        p.   cm.
    Includes bibliographical references and index.
    1. Bears—North America. 2. Bears—North
America—Pictorial works. 3. Bears—Behavior.
I. Ashworth, William, 1942–   . II. Title.
QL737.C27W64   1991
599.74′446′097—dc20   91-12087
                                        CIP

ISBN 0-517-58498-0

10 9 8 7 6 5 4 3 2 1

First Edition

Contents

A young brown bear
watches alertly for
salmon in the rapids of
the McNeil River,
Alaska.

Acknowledgments

Art Wolfe would especially like to express his gratitude to bear biologist Larry Aumiller for providing guidance and friendship during Art's many travels to the McNeil River Bear Sanctuary on the Alaska Peninsula.

William Ashworth would especially like to thank J. David Siddon of Grants Pass, Oregon, for his kind assistance in this project. A former Disney cinematographer, Dave Siddon has been reaching out to injured wild animals with his Wildlife Images animal rehabilitation center for more than seventeen years. He has probably raised and released more orphaned bear cubs than any other single living individual, and his compassion for these animals, his dedication to their well-being, and the deep fund of practical knowledge he brings to his work are certainly without peer.

Others whose help proved valuable include William Ashworth's wife, Melody (for her training and expertise in mammalian ecology as well as her moral support); Art Wolfe's staff, Mel Calvan and Margo Bernard; and also Rodney Badger, of the Southern Oregon State College faculty; Anne Richards, of the SOSC library; Bryan Frink; Max Gartenberg; Ron Mock; and Larry and Delores James.

Opposite: Two second-year brown bear cubs exhibit stress as several adult brown bears fish for salmon in close proximity to their mother. Mikfik Creek Valley, Alaska.

Overleaf: A brown bear mother leads two half-grown cubs toward the water at McNeil River Bear Sanctuary, Alaska.

BEARS
Their Life and Behavior

A large brown bear
paces along the edge of
Alaska's McNeil River
estuary at sunset.

1
BEARS
IN
THE
NIGHT

As a natural history writer, living and working in bear country for over twenty years, I am supposed to know something of bears; but this particular bear had me thoroughly spooked. We were camped, my wife and seventeen-year-old daughter and I, in an unimproved Forest Service campground at Colter Pass, just outside the northeast corner of Yellowstone National Park in extreme northern Wyoming. We had reached the place right before sunset, driving up from Cooke City in the long yellow light that lingers before twilight in the high Rockies. The day was fading fast. And there was the bear. Ambling down from the little knoll south of our campsite less than five minutes after we arrived, he walked directly through our camp—passing between my daughter and the car, a space of less than thirty feet—crossed the road, cruised past another camper's tent, and disappeared over the small open rise to the west. Darkness, uninterrupted, continued to descend.

My daughter was ecstatic. Moving carefully to keep a tree trunk between herself and the bear as a margin of safety, she had watched the animal approach to within about fifteen feet. "I've never been that close to a large wild animal before," she said happily. My own reaction was a trifle less overjoyed. Bears are normally shy animals that avoid human contact, often at considerable energy cost to themselves. They are remarkably adept at staying out of sight. A bear as casual about cars and tents and people as this one was clearly habituated to humans and human things—and a habituated bear is a dangerous bear. Virtually all bear attacks in the United States in the past ninety years have been attributable to habituated bears. Night was falling, and we were going to spend it in a thin-walled nylon tent with a habituated bear prowling about.

I knew the statistics: that in the entire United States there have been only thirty-two documented fatalities caused by black bears—which this one was—since 1900; that a National Park visitor is about 300 times more likely to be killed in a car accident in the park than by a bear. I knew these things—intellectually. But when faced with bears in the night, knowledge is no match for imagination. Rationally, you may be perfectly aware that bears almost never attack humans without provocation; emotionally, you *know* you are going to be eaten. We washed the table down thoroughly after dinner and put all our food, and everything that smelled like food, in closed metal containers inside the car, and before I fell fitfully asleep I placed a large knife within easy reach beside my head.

The human race has always been schizophrenic about bears. We are at once fascinated and repelled by them: we love them and fear them at the same time. We rejoice in their wildness

Above: Brown bear tracks stand out clearly in the silt at the edge of the McNeil River. The top track is a hind paw; the bottom, a front paw.

Opposite: A rare kermode bear peers from an alder in the northern Coast Range, British Columbia, Canada. Also known as the "ghost bear," the kermode is a white phase of the common black bear.

but sleep with knives near our heads. Like my daughter, we love to see them near us, but we want that tree between us and them just in case.

Bears inhabit every child's crib, but they also people our nightmares. There are Teddy bears and Paddington bears and Winnie-the-Pooh, but there are also the bears of Goldilocks and Grizzly Adams—bears of the wild, great hulking monsters that rise up suddenly out of our psyches to worry and devour us. We worship the creatures, but we prefer to do it at a distance. I live in the Bear Creek Valley, beneath a mountain called Grizzly Peak, in the shadow of a range called the Siskiyous, which means "bob-tail" in the Native American language of the region and may easily have referred to the local bears. (Most so-called primitive peoples use circumlocutions of this type to talk about bears because to speak the bear's true name is to evoke its power.) The local high school football team is called the Grizzlies. The last true grizzly was exterminated from the region in 1891.

Bears disappear in the winter, crawling into holes in the earth and slipping into a state resembling death, from which they burst forth in the spring, scattering clods and snow, renewed and vigorous. To this event can be transferred much of our own craving for resurrection. Ethnologists can trace for you today the scattered remnants of a bear cult, worldwide in distribution and remarkably uniform in its particulars, that probably dates from the time that early humans, expanding out of Africa, first encountered bears in the mountains of what is now the Middle East, 100,000 years or more ago. Still actively practiced at least as recently as 100 years ago in regions as remote from each other as Scandinavia, Quebec, and northern Japan, the bear cult ritual involved the sacrifice of a

Opposite: Alert brown bear cubs-of-the-year keep tabs on the photographer from the grass beside the McNeil River, Alaska.

A nervous brown bear warns the photographer away.

Brown bear subadults wrestle playfully in the McNeil River during a pause in fishing activity.

captive bear, either taken from its winter den or hand-raised from a cub; prayers to the dead bear for forgiveness; ceremonial dances which mimicked its movements; the ritual consumption of its flesh at a feast to which its soul was usually invited by setting a place for it at the table; and taboos on the consumption of certain parts of the animal by certain classes or sexes. Often the house where the feast was celebrated had a special doorway through which the body of the bear was passed, and which would be used for no other purpose during the course of the year.

The most widespread and longest-lasting part of the ritual involved the bear's skull, which was severed from the body and mounted in a raised location, on a pole or on the wall, where it could observe the ceremonies and make certain that they were carried out correctly, as well as serving as a focal point for veneration. Evidence of this portion of the ritual has been found in cave deposits at least 30,000 years old in central Europe, and it seems almost certain that the modern practice of mounting trophy heads on walls derives at least indirectly from it. Many of the ancient rituals must have been uncannily similar to those of our own day. Those 30,000-year-old European bear skulls had their teeth filed down in a distinctive, clearly ritualistic pattern. The same odd practice was observed as recently as the turn of this century in remote villages in Scandinavia and Siberia.

Or consider the Big Dipper—otherwise known as the Great Bear. When European explorers first reached the shores of what they chauvinistically referred to as the New World, they found native peoples who not only had named a group of stars "The Bear" but had attached this name to precisely the same part of the sky that the Europeans had. Since there is nothing particularly ursine about the actual appearance of those stars, the logical conclusion—accepted today by most anthropologists—is that the name arose many thousands of years ago somewhere in Eurasia and was carried around the world in both directions, arriving in North America with its Native American settlers during the closing years of the last Ice Age. As additional evidence, one can point to the fact that in virtually every culture where this constellation is recognized, the bear in the stars is called the "Great Bear" and is depicted with a long tail. No living bear has a long tail, but the cave bear—an immense Eurasian species whose huge size dwarfed all modern bears—did. The constellation appears to have been named for the cave bear. The cave bear has been extinct for 10,000 years.

(Or perhaps not quite extinct? Rumors persist of a race of immense bears that dwell on the Kamchatka Peninsula, the wild Siberian appendix that forms the western shore of the Bering Sea. Those who claim to have glimpsed them state that they are definitely not European brown bears: they are much larger than the local browns, their heads are shaped wrong, and their fur is solid black. A remnant population of cave bears? No scientist would dare to speculate on the basis of such flimsy evidence, of course; but no romantic can afford not to.)

During medieval times, the bear became a symbol for Christ's resurrection, weaving the bear-cult imagery intimately into the tapestry of Christianity. Bears were depicted holding up the sarcophagus of Christ, and bear's head and bear's claw images were worked into the illumination of religious manuscripts. Candlemas, the Christian feast of lights that celebrates the purification of the infant Jesus, appears to have been based on a Roman holiday which itself was derived from one of the early bear-cult rituals: bears figured prominently in the early celebrations of this day, and it is still called "Bear's Day" in parts

Brown bear cubs follow a well-established bear trail through the taller alders growing along Mikfik Creek. Sudden encounters with bears in dense foliage are dangerous.

of eastern Europe. A remnant of this persists in our own current secular Candlemas celebration, now known as Groundhog Day. Originally, the creature said to come out of its den and observe its shadow on Candlemas Day was the bear, not the groundhog.

Parallel to this pattern of bear veneration that has existed since long before history was thought of, however, there has always also run a deep undercurrent of ridicule, abuse, and destruction. Primitive peoples may have reverentially refrained from speaking the bear's name, but the nicknames they used in its place were often anything but reverential —"old honey-foot" and "old shaggy-bottom" being among the kinder ones. Medieval Europeans linked the bear to Christianity and called their heroes after it—the legendary King Arthur of England derives his name from the Greek word *arctos,* which means both "bear" and "north"—but they also made it a clown in their circuses, prodded it into lumbering, buffoonish dances, and practiced the so-called "sport" of bearbaiting, in which dogs were set upon a captive bear on a chain and allowed to maul and worry it to death.

We still see this same range of attitudes. Filmmakers elicit our sympathy as they turn bears into furry humans, Smoky the Bear admonishes us sternly to prevent forest fires, and Pooh Bear invites us in for a little smackeral of something; but hikers and campers still fear bears, animal damage control officers still trap and shoot them, and hounders—the modern equivalent of bearbaiters—still track them down, tree them, and turn their dogs loose to tear them apart. In Montana, whose 650-some-odd grizzlies form the only significant population of this endangered animal south of the Canadian border, there are strong and recurrent efforts to delist the species—to take it off the U.S. Endangered Species list —so that it may be trapped and hunted and hounded once more, so that livestock in the areas where the great bear lurks can be protected, so perceived threats to human safety can be eliminated. The ranchers who push the delisting maintain that desire to preserve the bear is a misguided result of what they call "eastern idealism." As one rancher put it to *National Wildlife* writer Jim Robbins not long ago, "if they [Easterners] were out here where the bear could take a bite out of them, they'd be just like us."

Who is more afraid of whom? A blue-gray glacier bear reacts warily to human intruders at Glacier Bay, Alaska.

Opposite: Twin brown bear cubs by the McNeil River stand upright to get a better view of other bears (or humans) who may threaten them.

An alpine meadow of yellow fawn lilies *(Erythronia)* near Logan Pass in Glacier National Park, Montana, is prime grizzly bear habitat. Summer recreational use of wilderness areas like this brings humans in close contact with bears, often resulting in trail closures.

Whence come these conflicting realities? How can a single creature be so thoroughly venerated and hated, feared and adored, at one and the same time—and often by one and the same person? Part of it, of course, is the animal's sheer, raw power: there is little in nature that can stop it aside from armed humans or an avalanche. Part of it is the strength of its intelligence—not so far inferior to our own—and part of it is clearly still the primitive symbolism of its springtime resurrection, the triumphant return from death that we seek for ourselves, not only healthy and whole but increased by the birth of cubs during the time of denning. I am convinced, however, that the real reason is "none of the above." The real reason, I think, for our ambivalent love-hate relationship with these creatures lies in the fact—often overlooked, usually ignored, and almost always misconstrued—that we and they are, from an ecological standpoint, virtually indistinguishable from each other.

Both of us are large, intelligent omnivores who can operate at any conceivable level on the food chain. Both of us like the same foods, in roughly the same proportions, and we seek them in the same locations. Both of us breed slowly and care aggressively for our young. Both of us, in short, occupy the same ecological niche—and there is no force on earth stronger than niche competition. The most fundamental rule of ecology, known as Gause's Principle, states unequivocally that two species cannot occupy the same niche at the same time. Where bears and humans interact, one of us must always lose.

And lately it has usually been the bears. Smaller and slower than they are, and endowed with far duller senses, we nevertheless have our brains and our opposable thumbs, and with these we can outcompete our ancient adversaries. The bear's share of the common niche is shrinking rapidly these days; the interspecies battle, which has raged nearly equally for thousands of years, has lately tipped decidedly in our favor. The war is just about over. We have won. Or have we?

Is eliminating our only serious competitor really a victory? Are we truthfully better off this way? Or are we actually poorer—poorer by that much less diversity, that much less challenge, that much less *reality*? Does the entire planet have to be made safe and sanitized for humanity? Do we really need—or even want—the whole thing?

A cinnamon bear (brown phase of the black bear) rests amid fiddlehead flowers (*Amsinckia intermedia*) in the foothills of the Sierra Nevada, California.

Pacing like a large cat, a polar bear near Churchill, Manitoba attempts to locate the source of a suspicious sound.

A young blond grizzly comes suddenly alert in northern Alaska's Jago Valley.

Opposite: A polar bear relaxes in the late afternoon light of an autumn day along the shores of Hudson Bay.

I think not. I think something important will have left us when the last bear disappears—something that helps define us as humans. The bear is the wild, shaggy side of our nature, the part that has not yet severed itself from our evolutionary past. It is, as Paul Shepard and Barry Sanders point out in *The Sacred Paw* (p. xi), "a kind of ideogram of man in the wilderness, as though telling of what we were and perhaps what we have lost." It defines wilderness for us, not so much because it is large and unpredictable and dangerous—though it is all these things—but because it lives the life we might have lived had we not chosen to come down out of the trees and put on evening dress. We may occupy our shared niche more efficiently than they do, but they occupy it more harmoniously. In bears' lives we see the paths our own ancestors did not take, and we are not always sure we appreciate their decision. "Science now hangs a radio transmitter on the bear's neck to track his movements," write Shepard and Sanders, "but we may ask who is really lost."

In the middle of the night my wife woke up and heard the bear snuffling about. Mercifully, she didn't wake me. The bear, finding nothing edible, moved on, as bears almost always do; in the morning there was not so much as a paw print to mark its passage through our lives. We were another nonincident, on which statistics are not kept. And so we repacked the car and drove on, past Beartooth Lake, over Beartooth Pass and down past Grizzly Peak to Interstate 90, where we turned east, away from Missoula, home of the University of Montana Grizzlies, toward distant Chicago, home of the Bears and the Cubs, and Boston, home of the Bruins. And several weeks and thousands of miles later, my daughter was still talking about the bear.

Sunset gilds the fur of this Hudson Bay polar bear as it heads out across the open tundra.

Overleaf: A brown bear boar mounts the much smaller sow, remaining coupled for approximately one hour. Just the preceding day, this same sow ran off her two third-year cubs. Mikfik Creek, Alaska.

2
TO
BE
A
BEAR

Opposite: A large brown bear grazes on succulent grasses in a damp Admiralty Island meadow. Though they are members of the order Carnivora, most bears' food preferences are largely vegetarian.

Bears are members of the order Carnivora, which also includes the cats, dogs raccoons, mustelids (weasels, otters, badgers, and skunks), pinnipeds (seals, sea lions, and walruses), and a few odd hangers-on such as the civets, hyenas, and mongooses. Their closest relatives appear to be the raccoons, from which they seem to have branched away approximately 39 million years ago somewhere in central Europe. In form they resemble large, round dogs, and they and the raccoons are generally placed with the dogs and their relatives in the suborder Canoidea. But here a contradiction begins to emerge. *Carnivore* means "meat-eater," and that is what dogs generally are. Bears are not. Like us, bears are omnivores, which means that they will eat just about anything in sight. Most of what is in sight is plants, so most of what bears eat is plant matter. What we have here, it turns out, are the largest, fiercest vegetarians on the planet.

Bears eat an astonishing variety of plants, and they eat them in large quantities. Nuts and berries are particularly prized for their high fat content (not, as is generally assumed, for their high protein content; more on this later), but almost any part of any plant will do. Grass is a favorite, particularly in the spring when the fresh shoots are coming up; dandelions are another, as are cattails, horsetails (a primitive water-loving plant which few animals besides bears can digest), and a variety of crop plants, especially corn, beans, squash, and potatoes. When all else fails, they may eat trees; not the whole tree, of course, but the cambium—the portion just below the bark which carries the nutrients down from the leaves—which they get at by stripping the bark away as high as they can reach and then shredding the cambium with their claws and pulling the shreds away with their teeth. Foresters in general hate bears: a single hungry bear can do more damage to a plantation of young trees than just about any other force in nature except fire or drought.

Bears eat meat, too, of course; in this they are pragmatic, taking only those animals which they can catch without a great deal of effort. Infants of any species, including their own, may become prey; so may old and infirm adults. Rodents may be swatted casually to earth and consumed in a bite or two. Migrating salmon and other anadromous fish form a staple for brown bears in the fall; domestic livestock and poultry are (often literally) sitting ducks. Nevertheless, the primary food of most bears—the polar bear and the sloth bear, a Southeast Asian species which lives primarily on ants and termites, are exceptions —is vegetables. In one typical study, produced by renowned bear experts David Hamer and Stephen Herrero for Parks Canada in 1983, the diet of grizzlies in Banff National Park was found to consist of an average of around 80 percent—and in some cases, close to 100 percent—plant matter.

And for the bear, this poses a significant problem. Their carnivorous ancestors spent many millions of years feeding primarily on meat, and from them bears have inherited what is in large part a carnivore's physiology. In particular, they have inherited a carnivore's gut. Plants are much harder to digest than meat is, and most plant-eaters have developed multichambered stomachs and long, convoluted intestines through which their food moves slowly, allowing digestive processes plenty of time to work. Bears have small, single-chambered stomachs, and their intestines—while they are somewhat longer than those of the average carnivore—are extremely short by herbivarian standards. They do not even have a caecum, the enlarged chamber at the junction of the small and large intestines that in herbivores—and in most omnivores, including us—acts as a sort of follow-up stomach into which undigested residues can be shunted for a little while to allow bacteria a chance to work on them.

The upshot of all this is that much of what a bear eats moves very rapidly through it and is deposited, still recognizable, behind the bear. The bear must therefore eat huge amounts of food to get a relatively small amount of nutrition. Because of this, bears are constantly hungry—"little more than appetites wrapped in fur," as wildlife rehabilitation expert Dave Siddon puts it. Their gluttony is legendary. It is not unheard of for an 800-pound bear fattening itself for winter dormancy to consume eighty or ninety pounds of food every twenty-four hours—the equivalent of a 200-pound human sitting down to three meals a day consisting of thirty large hamburgers each.

All this, by the way, has a certain advantage for biologists, who usually must study an animal's diet by examining its feces. With most animals, laboratory examination is necessary before positive identification of food residues in the feces can be made. Not so

Above and opposite: Black bear cubs at Bartlett Cove (Alaska) and in the Cascade Mountains (Washington State) show similar tastes for the leaves of low-growing shrubs.

with bears, who often seem to have merely borrowed a food for a little while. Not long ago, my wife and I came upon a number of bear scats while hiking on the little mountain behind our house. Obviously made by two separate bears—or by one bear at two separate times—they consisted of two radically different types. One set of scats looked like groups of red marbles loosely glued together; it was composed almost entirely of madrone berries (if it is true that you are what you eat, this bear was clearly a madrone tree). The other set was made of amorphous blue-black lumps that, when prodded apart, turned out to be whole plums, their skins wrinkled but intact. There were no plum trees in the vicinity. We could only conclude that the bear must be going down into town at night and raiding people's backyard fruit trees under cover of darkness.

And this turbocharged peristalsis, despite its obvious drawbacks, also conveys some significant advantages to the bears. As Stephen Herrero has pointed out, the fact that a bear's food passes through its gut so rapidly means that it wastes very little time in digestion. A standard-model herbivore bolts a large quantity of food and then goes and lies under a tree and chews its cud or sleeps while the food is digested. A bear bolts a large quantity of food and then keeps eating. The need for space to put more is taken care of quite nicely by the speed at which what is already in the system races through. This means that when the bear comes upon a cache of high-quality food, it does not have to pause partway through but can keep eating until the food is gone. It is far less likely to lose some to the competition.

Left: A bear-killed tree on Kodiak Island, Alaska. Hungry bears may pull the bark off trees to get at the nutrient-filled cambium layer beneath. Still others destroy a tree while simply sharpening their claws, referred to as *girdling*.

Right: Catching the scent of an approaching grizzly, a moose in Denali National Park (Alaska) prepares to flee. Note the raised hair on the back of the neck, which is a sign of stress. Though their diet is primarily plant matter, bears are true omnivores and will eat meat when they can capture it.

If a bear's gut is still largely the same as that of its carnivorous ancestors, however, the rest of the bear is certainly far removed. Its anatomy and physiology are superficially similar to those of a dog or weasel, but the differences in detail are profound.

Chasing ground squirrels, a Denali Park grizzly shows its great speed. Bears can run about twice as fast as humans over short distances but lack the endurance necessary for long pursuits.

The animal's molars are a case in point. In most carnivores—including the bear's distant ancestors—the molar teeth are carnassial, which means they are designed for shearing. In bears, as in us, the molars are occludal, which means they are designed for crushing. But where on our molars the broad occludal surfaces are composed of a regular pattern of cusps and hollows very similar to the teeth of herbivores (compare your molars to those of a horse someday), those of the bear are composed of an essentially random series of wrinkles and ridges, as though the shearing blades of a carnivore's molars had been stretched out and bent back on themselves a number of times—which is, in an evolutionary sense, precisely what happened.

Like a dog, a bear has long, powerful legs. Unlike a dog, those long legs end in plantigrade feet. A dog walks on its toes *(digitigrade)*, giving it a springier stride (the ankle as well as the knee flexes fully with each step) and concentrating its energy into a very small footprint—both of which improve its running speed. A bear places its feet down flat when it walks. Its feet, in fact, look remarkably like ours, with a row of five short toes, a broad, flat sole, and a narrow heel separated from the sole by a moderately high arch. Even the proportions are right. These are feet that are clearly adapted to a life of browsing rather than pursuit. But if you have the idea from this and from the animal's familiar slow, shambling gait that it cannot run fast, watch out! Bears can run about twice as fast as humans and can, in fact, outrun racehorses over short distances. It is not lack of speed that keeps the bear from being an efficient predator, but lack of endurance. Pound for pound, a bear exerts nearly twice as much energy as a human to do the same amount of work. No one knows just why.

Columbian ground squirrel *(Citellus columbianus)*.

Bears inhabit a sensory world that is fundamentally different from ours. We are sight-oriented animals, depending principally on the extremely fine discriminatory power of our vision. Bears are scent-oriented: they determine their path through the world largely by determining what it smells like. For all mammals, the acuity of the sense of smell depends primarily upon the size of the *olfactory mucosa*, a specialized area of mucous membrane located in the nose. In humans, the olfactory mucosa normally totals less than a square inch in area. In the average bear, it may be one hundred times that much. If the wind is right, a bear can smell you coming when you are still over a mile away. Bears have been known to detect the odor of rotting carrion from as far away as ten miles. "A pine needle fell in the woods," goes an ancient Native American saying. "The eagle saw it. The deer heard it. The bear smelled it."

Despite its strong reliance on its nose, however, a bear's other senses are as good as or better than our own. Bears can pick up the sounds of normal human conversation over a distance of nearly a quarter of a mile, and will usually come alert at the click of a camera shutter half a football field away from them. Their hearing, like that of a dog or cat, appears to range well up into the ultrasonic frequencies (blowing one of those "silent" dog whistles in bear country is probably not a particularly good idea). Their vision is also acute. I am aware that this flies in the face of popular wisdom, but it happens to be true. Their shape and color recognition ability is excellent—better than that of chimpanzees and other close human relatives. In a series of experiments in the mid-1930s, it was proved that

Above: Spawning sockeye salmon swim up Hanson Creek in the Wood River Lakes region of Alaska.

Opposite: Each summer the abundant salmon provide easy picking for the region's resident brown bear population.

Black bears, unlike brown bears, seem to prefer fishing by remaining as dry as possible. They will often catch exhausted fish that float near the water's surface.

European brown bears—the same species as our grizzlies and kodiaks—can visually recognize humans that they know from more than 300 feet away. The myth of the bear's nearsightedness probably stems from its strong desire to get all the information possible about any new situation it finds itself in—which means that it will almost always try to smell and feel things as well as see them before reaching any conclusions about them. A bear confronted with a strange human will usually rear up on its hind legs and start carefully testing the air with its nose. That is not because it can't see you well enough, but because it can't smell you well enough. Smell—as I said before—is the bear's most reliable means of getting information about the world, and the bear knows it. This does not mean that the bear's vision is worse than ours, only that its sense of smell is far better.

A bear's lips are extremely sensitive, and—unlike those of most Carnivora—are completely detached from the gums, making them highly mobile. When a bear "snuffles" a strange object, it may be feeling it with its lips as well as smelling it. I have watched bears in captivity affectionately kissing each other on the mouth, as humans would; there is no record of this in the wild that I am aware of, but it probably happens.

Their paws are also highly tactile. Like cats (or humans), bears do a lot of poking, prodding, and manipulating of strange objects in their environment to obtain information about them. The clumsy appearance of those long-clawed front paws is misleading: a bear's foot pads are highly sensitive, and its awesome-looking claws are actually delicately manipulatable tools. The animals can easily pick up tiny objects such as berries or feathers by grasping them between two claws, and can even rotate them or pass them from "hand" to "hand." In at least one well-documented instance, a bear escaped from a locked cage by picking the lock with one carefully maneuvered claw.

Infant bears are born in a state that in birds would be described as *altricial:* blind, hairless, and helpless, they are able to do little more than breathe, suckle, and defecate. Developmentally they are more like marsupial young than those of a normal placental mammal. (Some idea of the primitive, almost embryonic state of these infants at birth may be obtained from their birth weight, which is typically only about $\frac{1}{625}$ of the weight of their mothers: if human babies and their mothers had the same relative proportions, either the babies would weigh less than five ounces—about the size of a chipmunk—or their mothers would have to average around two and one-half tons each.) This stage of development is consistent with a gestation period of about three months. Bear pregnancies, however, last roughly eight months, from the normal mating period of early summer (usually June) to the birth of the cubs in January or February. What happens during those extra five months?

The answer, as it turns out, is very little. A fertilized bear ovum starts developing normally, splitting several times like that of any other animal until it has become a small sphere of undifferentiated cells—and then, at about the point this cell body (known technically as a *blastocyst*) would normally implant in the wall of the uterus and begin the process of cell differentiation, development suddenly ceases. Several months of free-floating suspended animation follow. In late October an as-yet-unknown trigger mechanism kicks in: the blastocyst implants in the womb, and development picks up just as abruptly as it ceased.

A brown bear mother and her three cubs-of-the-year bask in the afternoon sun at Mikfik Creek, Alaska. Bear litters can range from one to five; delayed implantation of the fertilized eggs means that the mother bear's body can tune litter size to nutritional conditions, with only those cubs coming to term which the mother's fat reserves appear to be sufficient to support.

Maintaining a vegetarian diet with a carnivore's gut means that this kermode bear, like all bears, must spend most of its time eating.

From an ecological standpoint, this process—known as *delayed implantation*—confers two distinct advantages. The first (and most important) of these is that it uncouples the time of mating from the time of birth, allowing each to take place at the optimal time of year for it to succeed. Bears mate in early summer because that is when they typically have the most time: they have regained most of the weight loss that takes place during winter denning but have not yet started the eating binge to fatten themselves for the start of the next denning season, so there is a little window of opportunity during which they can afford to slack off their typical frenetic feeding pace—foraging for food normally occupies about 90 percent of their time—and pay a little attention to the opposite sex. And bears give birth in late January or early February because that is during the middle of denning. The underdeveloped cubs are able to continue their development in the shelter and privacy of the den, which is only a little less protected from weather and other animals than is the womb itself.

Second—and nearly as important—delayed implantation means that the bears are able to practice an unconscious but highly effective form of birth control. There are typically three to five blastocysts floating around in a female bear's womb during the summer and early fall. If the feeding has been particularly good, all of them may implant; if it has been only average, just one or two will continue their development. During times of severe food shortage, all of the young may be jettisoned, allowing the mother to devote all her resources to keeping just herself alive. In early summer there is no way to predict which pattern will be needed. By late October the body knows.

You may have noticed that I have referred to the bear's winter dormancy, in the preceding paragraphs as well as elsewhere in this book, as "denning" rather than as "hibernation." That terminology reflects the scientific uncertainty that continues to surround this extremely basic and well-known bear activity. A bear's winter sleep does not match the typical pattern of hibernation. Its body temperature remains at near-normal levels; its metabolism is banked high enough that it does not remain torpid when disturbed, but becomes very awake—and very dangerous—within a matter of a few minutes. "Normal" hibernators cannot do that.

But if the bear is not hibernating, it is not simply sleeping a lot, either. Its heartbeat and breathing rate slow dramatically; its kidneys and digestive tract essentially shut down altogether. From the time it enters the den—usually in mid-November—to the time it leaves three to six months later, the bear will not eat, drink, urinate, or defecate.

How this feat is accomplished is not entirely clear. Defecation, of course, is not necessary if you don't eat, but most bears appear to go out of their way to make sure it won't happen by seeking out and consuming, shortly before crawling into the den, some indigestible material that will form a hard plug in the anus (when they wake up in the spring, their first order of business is usually to find some food, such as cascara, which can act as a good laxative). Urination is another matter entirely. The function of the kidneys is to remove waste materials from the bloodstream. Most of these waste materials are by-products of the basic reactions of metabolism rather than nonessential chemicals absorbed from the gut. If an animal is living at all, its kidneys have to produce urine. What does the bear's body do with it for six months?

The answer seems obvious: the urine gets reabsorbed. But this "answer" only raises further questions. If a hibernating bear is continuously reabsorbing its urine, why doesn't

Lolling beside the McNeil River, a brown bear shows off the soles of its feet. Bears are plantigrade, which means that they walk on the whole foot (like humans) rather than just the toes (like most other animals).

it die of uremic poisoning? If the bladder is just putting back into the blood all the wastes the kidneys are removing, why aren't they building up to toxic levels? Part of the reason seems to be that the bear is able to minimize its production of urea by metabolizing primarily fats and other carbohydrates, which contain no nitrogen and so do not result in uric acid formation. (This may also explain why it can get by without drinking: the by-products of carbohydrate metabolism include enough water to replace that lost to respiration, so even without water intake the bear is unlikely to die of dehydration.) But some nitrogenous wastes are going to be produced anyway, if only when cells wear out and die —a daily occurrence in all living creatures. Clearly the bear has some means of detoxifying urea either in the bladder or the bloodstream, but no one has been able to figure out just what it is. Kidney researchers would give a great deal to know: if the process could be simulated in humans, it would eliminate the need for artificial dialysis in patients whose kidneys have failed. That whole painful process could become a museum exhibit.

And how does the bear survive for six months on fats and carbohydrates alone, anyway? That is another thing we do not understand. Proteins—the basic building blocks of all living material—are formed primarily from a group of twenty nitrogen-based compounds called *amino acids*. The nitrogen necessary to form these acids cannot be obtained from fats and carbohydrates because they contain none. Where does it come from? Where, for that matter, do the amino acids themselves come from? Most animals cannot manufacture all that they need, but must obtain some of them—called *essential amino acids*—directly from the plants and animals they eat. As a class, the Carnivora require a higher

Opposite: Though the photograph is shot from a long distance with a powerful telephoto lens, this brown bear along Mikfik Creek is fully aware it is being observed. Despite its reputation for nearsightedness, a bear has eyesight as good as or better than that of humans.

It is difficult to tell whether this kermode bear is eating alder twigs or merely breaking them in an act of displaced aggression toward the photographer.

Bigfoot? These brown bear tracks at Icy Bay, Alaska, are strikingly humanlike, right down to the narrow heel and raised arch and the linear arrangement of the short toes.

number of essential amino acids than any other group of living things. How do the bears get by without them for six months out of each year? The mystery is only deepened by pointing out that for some bears, "six months" can be extended to "almost all of the time": polar bears, which live primarily by catching seals, often eat only the seal's blubber, leaving the rest of the carcass for scavengers, and the common black bear is well known for its preference for honey and other carbohydrate-rich foods; and I have already noted how the typical ursine attraction to nuts, seeds, and berries seems to be for their carbohydrate value rather than their protein content. (Bears do not easily digest solid proteins, anyway; they appear to obtain virtually all of their plant proteins during the short period in the spring when the plants are producing these substances in liquid form.) The animals seem to be able to recirculate much of their nitrogen instead of eliminating it in body wastes as others do, so that they need to consume only a minimal amount. Again, no one knows just how.

An animal that lives almost exclusively on saturated fats such as seal blubber and its own subcutaneous fat layer should suffer from severe cholesterol buildup. Bears don't. Why? What keeps their arteries clean? During normal activities a bear's blood cholesterol levels are about the same as those of a healthy human; during winter dormancy they climb to as much as twice that. A human with those readings would be a prime candidate for a heart attack. How do bears avoid them? The answer begins to approach being a litany: no one knows. One tantalizing clue lies in the fact that bears almost always concentrate their excess fat storage in their hips and thighs. Humans who put on weight in this manner—known as the gynoid pattern—do not commonly develop heart disease, either. Why not? The study of bears may eventually provide us with the answer.

To be a bear thus turns out to be a creature that is a bundle of walking contradictions: a carnivore that lives primarily on vegetables, a hibernator that does not hibernate, a big fierce animal whose claws—though they will function very nicely as claws, thank-you—turn out to be useful primarily as fingers. But though all this serves us well as a general description of bearishness, it does not tell us very much about the spirit of the animal. For that we must turn to literature, perhaps John Muir:

> He made a telling picture standing alert in the sunny forest garden. How well he played his part, harmonizing in bulk and color and shaggy hair with the trunks of the trees and lush vegetation, as natural a feature as any other in the landscape. . . . We stood staring at each other in solemn silence within a dozen yards or thereabouts, while I fervently hoped that the power of the human eye over wild beasts would prove as great as it is said to be. How long our awfully strenuous interview lasted, I don't know; but at length in the slow fullness of time he pulled his huge paws down off the log, and with magnificent deliberation turned and walked leisurely up the meadow, stopping frequently to look back over his shoulder to see whether I was pursuing him, then moving on again, evidently neither fearing me very much nor trusting me. He was probably about five hundred pounds in weight, a broad, rusty bundle of ungovernable wildness. . . .
>
> . . . I should like to know my hairy brothers better.
>
> —*My First Summer in the Sierra*, 1911

All senses alert, a polar bear checks out an intruder. It is now thought that bears stand upright primarily to improve their ability to catch faint smells rather than to see or hear better.

Overleaf: Even brown bear cubs are able to stand with perfect balance. Mikfik Creek, Alaska.

Top: Brown bear, McNeil River, Alaska.

Bottom: Waist-deep in the McNeil River, a brown bear plays with a stone it has picked up off the riverbed. The ability of bears to manipulate small objects is almost as good as that of primates.

Far right: Surrounded by a cloud of fluttering gulls, a brown bear and a bald eagle face off over a salmon amid the streamside sedges along the McNeil River.

Overleaf: A black bear is nearly lost in the shadows of large boulders along Anan Creek, in southeastern Alaska.

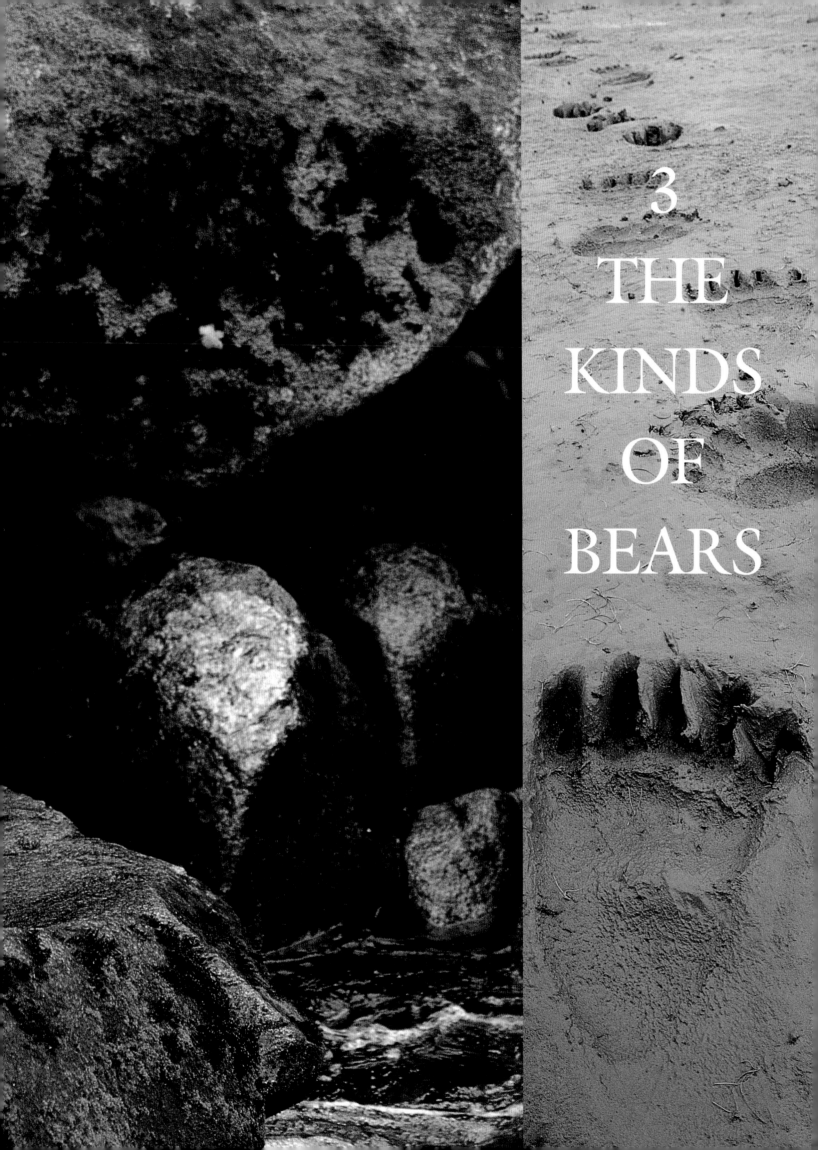

3
THE
KINDS
OF
BEARS

When C. Hart Merriam—the distinguished American naturalist and director emeritus of the United States Bureau of Biological Survey—published his monumental *Review of Grizzly and Big Brown Bears of North America* in 1918, he divided them into eighty-six separate species. Today's scientists recognize only one species of brown bears. This discrepancy can serve as an index to the confusion surrounding the relationships among the world's living bears: even today, with the tools of DNA comparison and computer analysis at hand, we are still unsure what to make of what we think we know. Worldwide, there are either seven or eight species of bears, divided into anywhere from three to six genera. Three of these species are found in North America: these North American bears are all members of a single genus. Or is it two? No one seems to be entirely certain.

The family trees of all living bears may be traced to a single genus, *Cephalogale,* which lived in central Europe in the late Oligocene, some 30 million years ago. *Cephalogale* was about the size of a raccoon, but its dentition and skeletal structure were similar to those of a modern bear. No members of this genus appear to have reached North America, but some of its relatives, the bearlike Hemicyoninae, did. The largest member of this group of proto-bears reached the size of small black bears, but they were rangier in build and were probably more predatory in their habits. All were extinct by the early Miocene era.

Cephalogale also died out in the early Miocene, but not before it had sired a descendant. *Ursavus,* which first appears in the middle Miocene—about 20 million years ago—is widely considered the first "true" bear. Roughly the same size as *Cephalogale* to begin with, *Ursavus* rapidly radiated into the numerous niches left vacant by the demise of the proto-bears plus a few that the earlier group had not found. Genera as well as species proliferated, some reaching nearly the size of the largest of today's brown bears. One genus, *Agriotherium,* apparently became the only bear to colonize sub-Saharan Africa: its bones have been found in a deposit near Cape Town, South Africa, dated at 5 million years ago. Another, *Indarctos,* migrated eastward through Asia and is thought by some paleontologists to be the ancestor of today's giant pandas. A third genus, *Tremarctos*—the so-called short-faced bears—split off somewhat later, reaching North America some 10 million years ago and radiating rapidly in this favorable environment, spawning several new genera as well as new species. Only one Tremarctine bear has survived into modern times: the spectacled bear, *Tremarctos ornatus,* found in the Andes Mountains of Chile, Peru, Ecuador, Colombia, and Venezuela. It is the only living South American bear and the only modern bear whose range lies primarily south of the Equator.

Opposite: Biologists currently believe that pandas represent a surviving early branch of the bear line. The theory that they are more closely related to raccoons has been largely discounted.

Earliest of the Ursids (modern bears) to diverge from the ancestral line, the black bears have now separated into four species, three in Asia and one in North America. This Malaysian sun bear *(Ursus malayanus,* formerly *Heloarctos malayanus)* is the smallest, most arboreal and most tropical of all living bears.

Note the pattern that has begun to emerge here. From *Cephalogale* on down, bears and bearlike animals have originated in Europe and migrated eastward through Asia to the Americas, radiating into various genera and species as they went. It is as though someone had dropped a stone into the bears' European gene pool sometime in the Oligocene: the ripples have been spreading outward ever since. The first wave, the Hemicyoninae, fetched up against the shores and damped out; the second wave, the Ursavines, is nearly gone, leaving two remnants—the giant panda and the spectacled bear—as slowly ebbing, widely separated eddies. The third wave is currently at its height. It consists of the Ursines—the bears that are members of, or have descended from, the genus *Ursus.* All remaining living bears are of this group.

The six living Ursine bears have been divided over the years into as many as six separate genera—one for each bear—but recent DNA analysis indicates that they are extremely closely related and should probably be considered a single genus. (There remains a great deal of dispute over this.) All can ultimately be traced to a single ancestral species, *Ursus minimus,* a tiny European descendant of *Ursavus* which appears in the fossil record approximately 2.5 million years ago. The closest living relatives of *U. minimus* are the black bears, of which there are currently four species, three in Asia and one in North America; these appear to have split off the ancestral stock almost immediately, and had achieved most of their present distribution and degree of separation by 1.5 million years ago. A somewhat later development were the brown bears, which consist of a single species worldwide, although they go by numerous local names: we know them most commonly here as grizzlies. Larger and slower-breeding than the blacks, the browns spread much

A kermode bear rests in a British Columbia meadow.

more slowly, and are not found in North America until the middle of the last ice age, some 70,000 years ago—not long before the first humans arrived. The most recent Ursine species separation took place only about 100,000 years ago, during the ice ages, when the polar bears split off from the browns. Like the other major differentiations in the bear line, this division took place in Europe, though the species has since migrated throughout the Arctic.

The entire living North American bear population thus consists of three closely related species belonging to a single genus. *Closely related,* however, does not mean *identical.* In fact, the characteristics of bears vary so much—not only among species but within the genetic confines of the species themselves—that it is no wonder that the early taxonomists were confused. We will get a sense of some of that confusion immediately as we undertake a closer examination of each species, beginning with what is undoubtedly the most familiar bear of all—the American black bear—which, despite its name, may be commonly seen in a great variety of colors, not only black but brown, white, gray, and even occasionally blue.

Black bears are the most widespread North American ursine species, ranging from Alaska (where this one was photographed) to California, Maine, and even Florida.

Opposite: European brown bears, like this one photographed in a Chinese zoo, belong to the same species as American brown bears and grizzlies.

T H E   B L A C K   B E A R

The black bear is known scientifically as *Ursus americanus,* which means simply "American bear." It ranges throughout the forested portions of the continent, from the Arctic treeline to Louisiana and Mexico, avoiding only the Great Plains, the southwestern deserts, and

Clambering over seaside rocks at Glacier Bay, Alaska, this American black bear is somewhat out of its normal habitat —the forest-edge environment represented by flower-rich alpine meadows such as the above in Mount Rainier National Park, Washington State.

the Arctic tundra. As bears go, it is medium-size, ranging from 200 to 800 pounds or so in weight, with most individuals weighing between 300 and 500 pounds. Males and females are about the same size. The head is somewhat elongated: the muzzle is large, and when it is seen in profile it forms a nearly continuous arc with the forehead, giving the bear a distinct "roman-nosed" appearance. The pelt is thick and smooth. The color, as we have already seen, is highly varied: eastern black bears are generally black, but western black bears can be just about any color. The brown phase, known as the cinnamon bear, is extremely common from the Rocky Mountains west, where it was once considered a separate species. That was before bear researchers noted that brown and black cubs were often part of the same litter. Cinnamon bear coats are occasionally grizzled and rough-pelaged, leading the animals to be mistaken for grizzlies. If you are tempted to make this mistake, bear experts say, look at the feet. Black bear claws are short and blunt, and are almost always dark-colored, no matter what the color of the animal is. Grizzly claws are much longer, and they are almost always light-colored. The difference is more distinctive than it sounds. Once you have seen the two types of claws side by side, you will never mistake one for the other again.

The other two principal color phases of the black bear are much less common than the blacks and the browns; they are also genetically distinct enough to be considered separate races and perhaps even separate subspecies. Each forms a geographically isolated population, separate from each other but close enough together that one suspects a single set of disruptions in the gene pool. The glacier bear *(Ursus americanus emmonsii)* is found

Opposite: This Glacier Bay black bear is probably utilizing tide pools for food, demonstrating its species' extremely adaptable diet.

Black bear cubs-of-the-year huddle against a tree in the Cascade Mountains of Washington State. The white patch of fur on the chest of the left cub is found on all Asian black bears and is fairly common in the American species as well.

Above and opposite:
A cinnamon bear in
the Sierra Nevada,
California. This bear's
rough pelage and rust-
brown coat might get it
mistaken for a grizzly,
but there is no shoulder
hump and the claws are
short and black.

Higher, more open
habitat, such as this at
the base of Canada's
Mount Robson, tends to
breed black bears of a
rusty brown color—
the variety known as
the cinnamon bear.

The glacier bear ranges from Glacier Bay (pictured) north to Yakutat Bay along the southeast coast of Alaska.

only on a small section of the Alaska coast, principally around Yakutat Bay, although some wander as far south as Glacier Bay. Its coat varies from gunmetal-gray through blue-gray to a genuine if rather dull blue, although the blue ones are becoming increasingly hard to find. The kermode bear *(U. americanus kermodei)* is even rarer than the glacier bear, occurring only around the northern arm of Douglas Channel, British Columbia—a coastal fjord —from Gribble Island near the channel's mouth to Kitimat at its head. Its fur is cream-colored, ranging in shade from reddish-yellow to nearly pure white: its eyes, nose, and claws are black. At first glance it may be taken for a polar bear that has wandered rather far from home, but it is considerably smaller than the great bear of the north, and its shape and habits are pure black bear, although it is shyer than most of its darker kin. The sight of this white bear-shaped shadow slipping quietly through the woods can be rather unnerving; it is no wonder that the Native Americans of the region referred to it as the "ghost bear."

All black bears—whatever their actual color—are primarily forest-edge creatures and are rarely found far from the shelter of the trees, although they apparently like the mosaic of woodland and small meadows that makes up the subalpine zone as much as we do and are often encountered there. (I have personally seen more black bears in subalpine meadows than in any other ecotype.) Their food preferences lean heavily toward mast (nuts and seeds), but they will eat just about anything edible, including carrion, insects, small rodents, greens, and berries and other fruits. They occasionally take livestock—particularly lambs and small pigs—though not as often as their reputation suggests.

Opposite and above: The silver-blue color of this glacier bear is typical of the animal, which is classed as a subspecies of the black bear.

The twilight-bathed landscape of the northern British Columbia Coast Range is the only place in the world that kermode bears, such as the one opposite, are found.

Looking a little like an out-of-place polar bear, a kermode bear—like the glacier bear, a subspecies of the common black bear—regards the photographer from the shelter of a shrub in northern British Columbia.

The color of a kermode bear's coat can range from yellow to almost pure white. This individual's rusty back is not uncommon.

The brown eyes and prominent black nose of this kermode bear indicate that its white coat is not caused by albinism but is a true color phase. This kermode relaxes in the cool water of a beaver pond.

THE BROWN BEAR

The brown bear, *Ursus arctos,* is the most widely distributed bear in the world: it is found throughout most of the northern hemisphere, from Europe (where it is the only bear) through northern Asia to western North America, where it once ranged as far east as Missouri and as far south as Mexico. Until about 1900, a small population of browns could even be found in the Atlas Mountains of northwestern Africa. *Ursus* means "bear" in Latin and *arctos* means "bear" in Greek, so what we have here is something called the Bear bear. The name is appropriate. No other bear combines so many of the traits we think of as bearish: the immense, bulky, lumbering shape, the long claws, the powerful forelegs, the ferociously short temper, and the appetite. Especially the appetite. John Muir was not far off when he wrote of this animal, "To him almost everything is food except granite."

Science currently recognizes fourteen subspecies of the brown bear. Twelve of these are found in Eurasia, where they are scattered all across the continent from the Pyrenees to eastern Siberia. The other two are in North America. One, *U. arctos middendorffi,* is found only on a few islands off the coast of Alaska and on one small portion of the mainland: it is distinguished principally by its immense size (a large male can weigh nearly a ton), but it also differs subtly from the rest of its kind in dentition and claw shape, and it is these rather than the size differential that make the subspecies designation warranted. It is known popularly as the kodiak bear. The other subspecies, *U. arctos horribilis,* goes by a wide variety of names in the various parts of the continent where it is found, but it is most commonly known by the name given to it by the explorers Lewis and Clark when they first encountered it on the upper Missouri River: the grizzly.

Grizzlies are smaller than kodiaks, but they are still extremely large animals: the weights of adults may range anywhere from 250 pounds to 1,300 or 1,400 pounds. Unlike black bears, they show strong sexual dimorphism, which means that males and females differ greatly in size. The differences seem to be related to their reproductive roles. Females generally stop growing when they reach sexual maturity, usually at five years; males continue to put on weight and length until at least the age of ten. The result is males that average about twice the size of their mates. This has caused no small confusion on the part of human observers: more than once, grizzly researchers have logged what looked like a mother and cub off in the distance, and have had to quickly change the notation when the "mother" suddenly mounted the "cub" and began copulating with it.

Brown bears differ from blacks in many ways besides the presence of sexual dimorphism. Their heads are proportionately larger and rounder; their muzzles are shorter, giving them a pug-nosed or "dish-faced" appearance. Their fur is longer and coarser, and there is a conspicuous hump of muscle tissue across their shoulders. A grizzly's toes lie in a straight line across the front of its foot, rather like ours: this is markedly different from the black bear, whose toes form an arc that resembles the relative position of our fingertips far more than it does our toes. The differences in the two species' claws have already been remarked upon. Deadly as they appear, the brown bear's claws do not seem to have developed as weapons, but as tools; combined with the enormous shoulder muscles in the hump, they turn the animal into an extremely efficient digging machine. This is probably related to the fact that one of their staple foods, throughout much of their range, is the roots of *Lomatium* (biscuitroot) and various other wild relatives of the carrot.

Opposite: A brown bear prowls the McNeil River estuary in Southwest Alaska.

Though the color of all brown bears is brown, the shade may range from blond to almost black.

Pages 72–75:
Migrating salmon are a
staple food of brown
bears, which often
develop superb fishing
skills. This one was
photographed at Brooks
River Falls, Katmai
National Park, Alaska.

The brown bears on
Alaska's Kodiak Island
are the largest land-
based carnivores on the
planet, and differ
enough from other
browns in small details
such as claw shape, skull
proportions, and
dentition to be classed as
a separate subspecies.

Above: A brown bear watches over her tiny cub-of-the-year near the McNeil River fishing grounds. Bears are among the animal world's best mothers.

Until their third year, brown bear cubs remain remarkably close to their mother, especially when in close proximity to other bears. McNeil River Brown Bear Sanctuary, Alaska.

Grizzlies are essentially open-space animals: they like plenty of room, and they like it unobstructed. They are most commonly encountered in the great sweeping timberline meadows of the western mountains, though they may also be found in the broad flat-bottomed valleys and along the wind-bared ridges and plateaus common to these heavily glaciated ranges. In historic times they ranged far out onto the Great Plains, and a few have recently reappeared there, in sheltered areas near the eastern boundary of Yellowstone National Park. A race known as the barren-ground grizzly has extensively colonized the tundra north of the treeline in northern Canada and Alaska; it is larger than the standard-model grizzly and considerably lighter in color, and some zoologists suspect that it may be a hybrid of the brown bear and the polar bear. The two species have mated in zoos and produced fertile offspring—offspring which look remarkably like barren-ground grizzlies.

Grizzlies were found in every western state when European settlers first pushed their way into this country. Today, confirmed populations exist south of the Canadian border only in Montana, Wyoming, and a few small areas of Idaho and Washington. Humans have been blamed, rightly, for this drastic reduction in the great bear's range; but one cannot help wondering if the animals were not living pretty close to the edge anyway. They like, as I said, open space, especially the type of open space found in the aftermath of recently retreating glaciers. Their spread into North America took place during and immediately after the ice ages, when much more of the continent would have shown these conditions. Some of the types of habitat they prefer is still found in all western mountains, but it has been shrinking for ten thousand years, and the bear populations have probably

Inland brown bears, commonly called grizzlies, are somewhat smaller than their coastal cousins.

Opposite: A blond Katmai National Park brown bear, her only cub killed by a large male, hunches disconsolately at the edge of the Brooks River.

The grizzlies of Denali National Park's Toklat Valley, known as Toklat blonds, are usually extremely light-colored.

Overleaf: Grizzlies generally prefer open country, like the autumn-splashed tundra of the Arctic National Wildlife Refuge, Alaska.

been shrinking with it. The arrival of humans with guns and fences was undoubtedly only the last of a long series of blows. Grizzlies were common in my portion of Oregon when the first white settlers arrived in 1852. By 1891—just thirty-nine years later—the last of the great bears was gone. That does not suggest an animal that was well fitted to its habitat and able to compete on anything approaching equal terms. Black bears are still found here in large numbers. The forest-edge environment they like remains common. The large open meadows preferred by the grizzly had largely disappeared before the settlers arrived.

THE POLAR BEAR

If brown bears are the most bearish of living bears, polar bears *(Ursus maritimus)*—despite their extremely close genetic link to the browns—are probably the least. The great white bears of the far north show some striking divergences from what are thought of as standard ursine characteristics. They are rangier than other bears, with longer legs and more powerful hindquarters; their muzzles are much larger than those of their more southern relatives, and contain a complicated network of nasal heat-exchanging passages that allows the cold polar air to be warmed somewhat by the bear's exhaled breath before it enters the lungs. Virtually all of the animal's time is spent either on the ice or in the ocean, and its feet have adapted to this life-style: the soles are covered with hair, and the toes are partly webbed. Those hairy soles are not just for warmth. On the slick ice they create a much more effective nonskid surface than bare skin would provide. The lesson has not been lost on humans: boots made for Arctic walking are now commonly constructed with hairy soles, and the principle has begun to be adapted for use on the footgear of those who must work on oily floors.

The greatest difference between this bear and others, however, is not in its physique but in its diet. Other bears are omnivorous, which means largely vegetarian—in the case of the brown bear, almost completely so. Polar bears have returned to the ways of their carnivorous ancestors. Their diet is almost exclusively meat, augmented occasionally by kelp and by the few hardy grasses and berries that grow in the high Arctic. They eat seabirds and their eggs, lemmings, Arctic foxes, beached whales, and other carrion—in fact, almost anything they find or can catch—but their staple diet is seals. In the North American Arctic, this means primarily ringed seals *(Phoca hispida)* and bearded seals *(Erignathus barbatus)*. Both of these fairly large seals are about the size of humans, and when we dress in sealskin parkas we look remarkably like them. Many authorities believe that it is our resemblance to seals, rather than the polar bear's inherent pugnacity toward us, that is behind most recorded polar bear attacks on people.

The return to carnivority has altered many aspects of the physique of this most specialized of bears. Their molars have redeveloped some of their lost carnassal characteristics—not completely (polar bears must still largely crush rather than rend the meat of their prey, a fact which allows researchers to determine whether or not a polar bear has been feeding on a particular abandoned carcass), but enough to allow the bear to get by with a nearly all-meat diet. The claws have shortened and sharpened, so that they resemble those of a cat more than they do those of other members of the bear family. The hind legs

Opposite: Grizzly bear, Arctic National Wildlife Refuge, Alaska.

Symbol of the Arctic, a
polar bear strides across
the ice at the margin of
Hudson Bay.

have lengthened to allow for greater mobility; the front legs and shoulders have retained the massive musculature of the brown bears, making them capable of enormous feats of strength. Polar bears can reach into the water and almost nonchalantly flip a quarter of a ton of seal onto the ice beside them with one paw. They have been observed to grasp a seal's head in their jaws, heave backward with their forelegs, and pull the animal right up through the breathing holes they make in the ice. A seal's breathing hole generally is less than a foot in diameter; the animals themselves average around two feet in diameter. In order to pass it through the hole, nearly every bone in the seal's body must be either dislocated or crushed.

Polar bears spend a lot of time in the water—their scientific name, *U. maritimus,* means "bear of the sea"—and they have developed a number of adaptations to assist them in this life-style. The partial webs of their feet have already been mentioned; they also have a well-developed diving reflex that causes their nostrils to close, slows their heartbeats, and temporarily shifts the metabolism of their muscle cells from aerobic to anaerobic (oxygen-using to oxygen-independent) when they submerge. (There are subtle differences between the polar bear's diving reflex and that of other seagoing mammals, enough to suggest that it may have developed out of the same set of physiological adaptations that other bears use for hibernation.) Their nictating membranes (the transparent "third eyelid" found on almost all vertebrates except humans) are different from those of other bears, and it has been suggested that they have been modified to act as an extra lens to help the bear see better underwater. The animals are excellent swimmers, and have been seen as much as 300 miles from land. Stroking with their front legs and steering with their hind feet, they can travel for long periods at speeds of up to eight knots. They can also leap out of the water a full body length—a skill that is very useful for climbing out onto ice floes.

A mystery that still intrigues scientists is just how polar bears manage to keep warm. We have learned just enough about the process to know how much we still don't understand. We know that the most obvious answer—the insulating ability of those long, thick coats of shaggy white fur—is only partly correct: polar bear hair is indeed a better insulator than that of other bears, but it is wettable (absorbs water easily) and loses much of its ability to retain warmth when the bear has been in the water for very long, leaving it vulnerable both to hypothermia in the cold polar seas and to intense wind chilling when it climbs out on the ice. Subcutaneous fat, or "blubber"? Again, the answer is maybe; polar bears do carry a thicker layer of fat beneath their skins than other bears do, but owing to a quirk in their life cycle—to be explained in a moment—they have reversed the typical bear pattern of summer activity and winter inactivity and are actually least well insulated by fat during the winter months, when the need for warmth is greatest. This pattern is counterproductive for use of the fat for warmth retention but precisely right for its utilization as food storage, and most scientists today believe that this is its primary role. But if neither fat nor hair is responsible for keeping the bear warm, what is?

Opposite: Unlike the dished-in face of the kodiak brown bear the polar bear has evolved a longer skull adapted for a more carnivorous diet.

There does not seem to be a single answer to this question, only a group of partial ones. An intriguing and little-known fact about these bears, for example, is that their skins are black. Black is the most efficient color for absorbing solar radiation and converting it to heat. This might seem irrelevant underneath all that white fur, but the fact is that the individual hairs of that fur are not white but transparent. Each hair actually is a highly efficient fiber-optic device, capable of conducting much of the solar radiation that strikes it right down to that black, radiation-absorbing skin.

Polar bears are semiaquatic animals who spend a great deal of their time in the water.

Opposite: Combining powerful shoulders and legs with partially webbed feet, the polar bear is able to demonstrate remarkable aquatic skills.

The hairs are also hollow. This means that even when the fur is soaked through and clinging to the skin it retains some dead-air space and hence some insulating ability, but this seems almost incidental to the hair's real function, which is infared blockage. In some not-yet-understood manner, the architecture of polar bear hair appears to be almost completely opaque to infrared radiation, short-circuiting what is for most animals a major source of heat loss. An animal with black skin should be radiating like crazy. Polar bears actually lose so little heat in this manner that snow will not melt on their fur, and they cannot be spotted at night by using the normal animal-location technique of infared photography. The only sign of a polar bear in infrared light is a small fuzzy region just in front of the nostrils—the animal's exhaled breath.

None of this helps very much in the water. Here, the bear appears to use the same technique practiced by human divers with wetsuits, utilizing the water's own high specific heat as a barrier to heat loss. If a layer of water is trapped next to the skin, it will draw heat from the body as it warms up—but once it is warmed to body temperature it will lose heat only very gradually to the environment surrounding it, thus effectively preventing any further body heat from being drawn off. Divers fill their suits with warm water for that reason. The bear's fur functions in much the same manner: water can soak through it down to the skin, but once it is there it cannot move very far. Once that layer of water next to the skin has been warmed up, most further heat loss stops—most, but not all; the process is not perfect. Odd as it may seem, wet polar bears can and do suffer from hypothermia, and will freeze to death if they are forced to stay in the water too long.

Polar bears, normally
solitary, interact rarely.
When males such as
these congregate along
Cape Churchill, their
mock battles end
harmlessly.

Black bears like the woods; grizzlies like the open spaces. Polar bears, it goes almost without saying, like the ice. But not *all* the ice: only ice meeting certain requirements. Though polar bear tracks have been found in the middle of the Greenland ice cap and on the solid sea ice less than 150 miles from the North Pole, these were apparently either aberrant individuals or very, very lost. Under normal conditions the bears stick very close to the coastline of the Arctic Ocean, rarely venturing more than fifty miles from it, either inland or out to sea. The reason is simple: this is where the seals live. In the winter, the bears hunt the seals, prowling the Arctic ice pack, searching for breathing holes or for the open leads that develop in sea ice even in the coldest of weather. In the summer the ice melts, the seals go away, and the bears go hungry. Polar bears do not den up during the winter; they cannot afford to, because that is when the most food is available. Instead, they are likely to build dens and curl up in them for much of the summer. The primary exception to this is pregnant females: they will often den for a few weeks during midwinter while their cubs are being born. They do not even approach a state of hibernation during this process, and the whole thing appears to be a holdover from their brown bear ancestors which has survived only because, as a practical matter, it provides a great deal of protection for the newborn cubs.

Because of their habitat-linked dependence on the Arctic coastline, most polar bears live at or above the Arctic Circle, in both North America and Eurasia. The one great exception to this rule occurs in eastern Canada, where the vast, Alaska-sized arm of the Arctic Ocean known as Hudson Bay penetrates far into the continent, nearly as far south as the 50th parallel. A thriving population of bears has penetrated along with the bay; 40 percent of the world's known polar bears now live in this anomalous setting far to the south of the rest of their species. In the winter they work the frozen surface of the bay. In the spring, they ride the disintegrating ice floes onto the shore and disperse southward over the tundra. High summer finds most of them in dens, concentrated in two locations: one near Churchill, Manitoba, and the other in what has recently become Polar Bear Provincial Park, 300 miles northwest of Moose Factory, Ontario. In September they emerge, ambling north toward the great bay again. Geography funnels many of them onto the Churchill Peninsula; by early October, more than 1,000 bears are clustered at the tip of the peninsula, waiting for the bay to freeze over, and for two months the little port city of Churchill, Manitoba, becomes the polar bear capital of the world. There are literally more bears in Churchill during this period than there are human residents. But there are not more bears than humans; along with the bears, the town is invaded by tourists overflowing its four hotels, which are booked months in advance. For approximately six weeks the town, the tourists, and the bears exist in uneasy triple harmony; then the bay freezes over. The bears and the tourists rapidly disperse, in opposite directions, leaving the village to winter and to peace.

Opposite: The thick fur of the polar bear provides such good insulation that snow on it is not melted by the bear's body heat.

When freeze-up comes to Churchill, polar bears and tourists both desert the village.

A polar bear wanders
through the spruce
woods near Churchill,
Manitoba, while waiting
for Hudson Bay to
freeze over.

4
WHERE
BEARS
LIVE

Sometime in the late 1950s, a church youth group out for an afternoon lark was exploring Allbright Cave, a small, isolated limestone cavern in Washington State's Okanagon country. They had been in the cave for an hour or so and were on their way out when somebody noticed the bear. Off in a corner of the large entrance chamber, apparently undisturbed by the shouts and laughter of the teenagers as they picked their way up and down the steeply sloping floor to the pit and tunnel complex that constitute the rest of the cave, a good-size black bear was slumbering peacefully through its winter dormancy. And as the suddenly much quieter teens squirmed rapidly out of the tight cave entrance, they might have been pondering this central truth: bears are where you find them. The dry, open ridges of the Okanagon are hardly typical black bear habitat. No one, obviously, had bothered to explain that to this particular bear.

Bears are the greatest pragmatists in the animal kingdom. Like all animals, they tend to go where the food is—and to a bear, food is nearly everything. Large and formidably muscled, they have few natural enemies—none, really, except each other and ourselves—and can thus do pretty much as they please, with no strong need for places to hide or inaccessible nooks to roost in. The combination of these two traits has led to an animal with extremely flexible ecological requirements. For most animals, the ecologist's term *preferred habitat* actually means *required habitat:* an animal forced to use an alternate habitat will suffer strongly and is likely to die. For bears, preferred habitat *is* preferred habitat. Black bears prefer deep woods and small meadows, but where adequate food exists they will happily live elsewhere, in the bayous of Louisiana or the suburban woodlands of New Jersey or even the near-desert ridges of northcentral Washington—provided, of course, that those near-desert ridges are adjacent to some of those world-famous Okanagon apple orchards, thank-you very much.

More than most animals, a bear's home is where the bear happens to be at the moment. Though they are largely solitary by nature and tend to avoid each other's company (there are exceptions; see the next chapter), they are not strongly territorial, and individuals often wander widely during the course of their lives. The old children's song about the bear that went over the mountain is based on observed reality. Bears are always going over mountains—or through forests, or along seacoasts, or *some*where. They are probably the most perambulating creatures on the planet. Yellowstone and Glacier national parks, for example, contain the only two remaining significant populations of grizzlies south of the Canadian border. Between the two parks lie approximately 250 miles of

Opposite: Form follows function: this koala—a marsupial—is completely unrelated to Northern Hemisphere bears, but it is strikingly bearlike in appearance and fills a similar niche in the Australian environment.

Pages 98–99: Polar bears trudge through an autumn snowstorm on the shore of Hudson Bay. Beaches are common travel corridors for these water-dependent bears.

Prime grizzly country, Alaska's Brooks Range spreads its treeless slopes in the Arctic National Wildlife Refuge.

forest and farmland and mountains where grizzlies are not supposed to be. But the bears are occasionally seen there anyway, and there is speculation that these may be particularly footloose individuals who are tired of life in one of the two parks and are going to visit Aunt June and Uncle Bob over in the other one. Black bears are less prone to wanderlust than grizzlies, but marked blacks have been caught over 100 miles from their original point of capture. Polar bears range over immense pieces of territory. In one documented case, a tagged polar bear was shot less than a year later but 2,000 miles away.

Most bears, however, stick within a relatively well-defined home range, if only because familiarity with their own turf makes it easier to find food there. For the fact is that, despite the uncanny sensitivity of their noses (grizzlies, to pick one example from many, are able to locate edible plant bulbs by scent while they are not only unsprouted but are buried by a couple of feet of crusty spring snow), a bear's principal tool for locating nutrition is its memory. It knows from experience where the best foods are and when they are likely to be ready to eat, and it can plan its travels accordingly. Bears do not for the most part just happen onto food; they make a planned circuit of known sites, most of them shared with other bears who are making their own separate but overlapping circuits. If they find a new site they will include it in the circuit the next time. If a site proves to be a bust they will probably give it a cursory look the next time anyway; if it continues to be a bust it will be crossed off the bear's mental list of grocery stores. If many sites come up busts, the bear will probably light out for new territory. A bear is no sentimentalist; it will take a full stomach over familiar terrain anytime.

So where bears live is not a specific piece of defendable turf, but a large network of activity sites—what biologists refer to as *biocenters*—connected by travel corridors. Each network is highly individualized to the particular bear that has created it; nevertheless a few generalities can be given. A black bear's home range is likely to include fruit- and nut-bearing trees, bee trees, berry patches, cattail swamps, damp meadows (for the grass they grow), and rotting logs (for the insects and grubs that inhabit them). Its travel corridors tend to be beelines (bearlines?) from one biocenter to another. Grizzlies also like food-bearing trees, berry patches, and damp meadows, but they prefer horsetails to cattails (for whatever reason, they consider these primitive plants—which most animals cannot even keep down, let alone digest—a great delicacy), like dry meadows for the plant bulbs they are likely to contain, and rarely make more than incidental use of rotting logs. They also make heavy use of fishing streams, especially during salmon-spawning season. Their travel routes tend to be along alder- and willow-choked stream bottoms or, where these are unavailable, up and down ridges. Both species will establish temporary biocenters at the carcasses of large animals (either ones they have killed or ones they have discovered), meadow-mouse colonies, and squirrel trees; both will also take full advantage of human-created biocenters such as garbage dumps, orchards, and unguarded livestock, especially those with young.

Black bears, on the whole more timorous than grizzlies, also require a range that includes a fair amount of hiding cover. Grizzlies are not much for hiding cover, but they (and the blacks) do require a good scattering of thermal cover—shade to shield them from the sun and brush and tree canopies to hold in the heat at night and during cold snaps. Neither species commonly takes shelter from the rain. They seem to like being out in it, perhaps because of the way it magnifies odors. (These are, after all, largely scent-oriented animals.)

Pages 104–106: A caribou herd grazes the foothills of the Brooks Range of the Arctic National Wildlife Refuge, watched by an interested grizzly.

A coastal black bear
stands amid beach
grasses in Southeast
Alaska.

Polar bears are, as usual, a special case. They occupy a constantly shifting, drifting, moving habitat, one in which a biocenter that provided a good lunch last month is likely to be halfway to Iceland today. Often the bears drift with these moving biocenters, riding the floes along with the seals that are their principal prey. At other times they will stay with a single piece of ocean, waiting for the moving biocenters to come drifting past them. Still, there remains a kind of grand, bearish cycle of biocenter and travel corridor to their lives: out onto the ice in the winter to feast on seals; back to shore at the spring breakup to eke out a living in a series of stationary but meager biocenters that include kelp beds, berry patches, lichen fields, and the occasional lemming colony or beached whale; following well-established travel routes to jumping-off spots such as the Churchill Peninsula; waiting for the seas to freeze and the cycle to begin again. Like their more southerly cousins, they take full advantage of any human-created biocenters that crop up in their territory. Garbage dumps in the far north are often centers of frenzied polar bear activity.

All three species require, as a matter of course, that their home ranges include good denning sites. Black bears are the least particular about this. To them, a "good" denning site is nearly anywhere they are not likely to be disturbed. Black bears have been found hibernating in an amazing variety of places, including natural caves and rock overhangs, enlarged fox dens, hollow trees, culverts, and the crawl spaces under occupied buildings. Occasionally they will simply curl up under a bush and "den up" right out in the open.

Grizzlies are far pickier. They usually either dig a den themselves or occupy one some other grizzly has dug in the past. Almost always the dens run horizontally into steep banks of grass-stabilized soil and are oriented so that winter storms will pile a large concealing and insulating drift of snow over the entrance. In any given area, all dens will be at about the same elevation and will often face the same direction. A final requirement is solitude: grizzlies are more vulnerable while they are denning than at any other time during their lives, and they do not bloody well want to be found. The encroachment of civilization into grizzly country is felt most destructively at the bears' den sites, and as the supply of sufficiently isolated and remote sites in a given area shrinks to nothing, the bear population is almost certain to disappear with it.

Polar bears may be the pickiest of all. They do not build dens and "hibernate" during the winter as other bears do, but pregnant females do fashion so-called maternity dens and spend several weeks in them, birthing and nursing their infants. These are almost always dug into snowdrifts backed up against rock or earth walls, and they almost always face south—and like the grizzlies' dens, they must be isolated from all creatures except other polar bears. These conditions are harder to meet than might appear. In all the world there are only seventeen known regions where polar bear maternal denning takes place. Five of these are in North America: in western Alaska on the coast of the Chugkchi Sea, in northern Alaska on the Arctic coastline, in Canada's Arctic Archipelago, and at two places just south of Hudson Bay, one about forty miles from Churchill, the other in Ontario's Polar Bear Provincial Park west of the mouth of James Bay.

Though they do not den up in the winter, polar bears do often enter a state resembling hibernation during the lean food days of summer. The dens built for this purpose are separate from the maternity dens, and are usually dug into soil banks that rest over permafrost. In this way the bear gets a firm floor and natural air-conditioning. The quagmire that results from the melting of the top layer of permafrost by the bear's body heat is easily handled by dragging in kinnikinnick.

Black bear cubs rest in a Washington State apple tree. Bears take full advantage of human-made biocenters such as orchards.

Taking a break from
fishing, a brown bear
sow, with her cubs,
drowses during an
afternoon rain shower.
Mikfik Creek Valley,
Alaska.

Thus far in this chapter we have concentrated on *habitat*—the type of terrain that bears prefer to live in. Where an animal lives, however, also includes its *range*—the actual geographic limits within which it is found. We have discussed range briefly for each of the three North American bear species in the previous chapter. Here I would like to broaden that discussion a bit to look at the range of bears as a family, to make some general observations on this topic, and to offer one tentative but extremely intriguing conclusion.

When the confirmed ranges of all bear species on the planet—past and present—are plotted on a single map, a striking pattern emerges. Virtually every square inch of the Northern Hemisphere has at one time or another had bears on it; but aside from the Andes Mountains of South America and that single anomalous 5-million-year-old proto-bear skeleton near Cape Town, South Africa, nothing in the Southern Hemisphere ever has. This means, obviously, that bears are strictly a Northern Hemisphere phenomenon, originating, evolving, and continuing to live almost exclusively in the northern half of the globe. It also means—less obviously—that there is a great deal of prime bear habitat in the Southern Hemisphere that has never had bears on it. In fact, there are two whole continents—Australia and Africa—that are completely bearless and always have been, at least for all practical purposes. On both of these continents there is much habitat of the type that bears like. Nature abhors an empty niche. What, in these two immense spans of territory, has taken the bear's place?

For Australia, the answer turns out to be relatively straightforward. Australia not only has no bears, it has no indigenous placental mammals at all except dingos (wild dogs)

Polar bears are the greatest ursine travelers: individual bears have been known to cover territories up to 2,000 miles long.

Opposite: Engaged in a bear's standard routine of biocenter and travel corridor, a glacier bear grazes for a while in a dry meadow and then moves on. Dundas Bay, Alaska.

Summer and autumn are the lean seasons for Manitoba polar bears, which cannot go out on the ice to hunt seals and must therefore take whatever they can find. These two bears are feeding on kelp washed up on the shores of Hudson Bay.

Polar bears, like others, often take full advantage of human-formed biocenters. These bears in the town dump in Churchill, Manitoba, seem unbothered by flying sparks from nearby garbage fires, which have badly singed their coats.

Opposite: Unlike its brown and black cousins, this polar bear will not hibernate during the winter snows, but will head out onto the frozen Arctic Ocean to hunt seals.

and humans, which undoubtedly arrived together well after both had completely evolved. In the absence of placental competition, the marsupial mammals—kangaroos, opossums, and their relatives—have radiated into all the available niches. Thus Australia has developed marsupial "bears"—the koalas. The correspondence is not precise—the entire niche structure of Australia is skewed, owing to its long separation from the other continents—but it is close enough, as anyone who has spent any time watching a koala can easily confirm.

Africa presents a considerably knottier problem. It has been connected to Eurasia through the Middle East and (off and on) through Gibraltar for most of recent geologic time, and its ecology is intimately bound up with that of the northern continents. It has a full complement of placental mammals, most of them closely related to Eurasian species and filling virtually identical niches. By all rights it should have bears. Where are they?

There is no confirmed answer to this question, but there are the beginnings of consensus behind a provocative hunch. There are no bears in Africa, most ecologists now believe, because they evolved too late, and when they arrived their niche was already full. The creature that had filled it was a descendant of ancient insectivores that had grown considerably and taken up very bearlike omnivorous ways. It was shaped much like a bear, but it was bipedal and had lost most of its body hair. It was, in short, *us.* We are the bears of Africa: large omnivores on plantigrade feet, eaters of the same food, fillers of the same niche. Brothers under the hairy skin. We owe our evolutionary lives to the fact that bears were slow to spread past the Equator. Perhaps this is a debt that we should begin at last to find the courtesy to repay.

Black bear, Dundas Bay,
Alaska.

5

WHAT

BEARS

DO

O n April 21, 1990, while conservationists around the world were celebrating John Muir's 152nd birthday and the British Commonwealth was marking Queen Elizabeth's 64th, Alaska's Mount Redoubt volcano got into the act by staging a little celebration of its own—a major, Mount Saint Helens–type explosive eruption that spewed an ash plume more than 30,000 feet into the cloudy spring skies over Lake Clark National Park. A crowded Dutch Air Lines (KLM) jumbo jet, all four of its engines clogged with ash, stalled and fell 13,000 feet before the pilots managed to regain partial power and limp to a landing in Anchorage. West Coast vulcanologists waited anxiously for the tremors to subside and the skies to clear, impatient to get to the mountain's caldera and observe the eruption's effects. They were not the only ones. When the first teams of scientists arrived at the caldera's rim, they spotted fresh snow—and fresh tracks. Bear tracks. One of Lake Clark's ursine inhabitants, perhaps rudely awakened from winter dormancy by the volcano's blast, had climbed 10,000 feet up the side of the mountain to peer inside and find out what the hell was going on in there anyway.

Bears are intensely curious. For a large omnivore with a carnivore's gut, intense curiosity is probably a necessary survival trait: that immense, shaggy body requires a huge amount of nutrition, and the bear must be constantly testing everything in its environment to find out which things are edible so that it can eat all of them. As Dave Siddon puts it, "food is more important than anything else to a bear, even sex." But the fact that these "appetites wrapped in fur" evolved their curiosity as a survival trait does not mean that they cannot use it for something other than mere survival. Bears are curious about everything, not just food. They spend most of their waking time exploring things—poking them, prodding them, turning them over, tearing them apart. When they find something that reacts in an interesting way to their prodding, they will prod it again. Gotta test; gotta find out; gotta *know*. Gotta know *now*. Paul Shepard and Barry Sanders's description of a bear as "a taciturn, churlish, hirsute little kid weighing 200 pounds" (*The Sacred Paw*, p. 39) is exactly correct.

Bears are extremely intelligent animals, with excellent memories, strong powers of observation, and good reasoning ability. Anecdotes that demonstrate these qualities abound. In Pennsylvania, a black bear entered a locked garage through an open window, opened a freezer, and made off with most of the meat that had been stored there (it didn't close the freezer after itself: most of the rest of the food spoiled). In Yosemite National Park, another so-called mugger bear (that is, a bear that obtains food by stealing from humans) discovered that the doors of a Volkswagen Beetle can be forced open, even when

Opposite: More curious than antagonistic, a polar bear approaches the camera. Polar bears often cover their black noses with their white paws to improve camouflage while hunting.

Pages 122–123: A brown bear sow with two cubs explore the shallow water at the top of the McNeil River Falls.

locked, by crushing the car's roof to increase the air pressure inside. It thereafter concentrated on mugging Volkswagens, destroying a number of them before being captured.

Canadian bear expert Stephen Herrero tells of a time he watched two black bear cubs play rocket ship with a small sapling. With both bears in its top the sapling would bend to the ground, but with the weight of only one it would stand straight: so if one cub hopped off while the sapling's top was bent over, the other would be shot rapidly upward as the little tree suddenly straightened up. Though the cubs' discovery of this little carnival ride was undoubtedly accidental, its continuous use for the rest of the afternoon was certainly on purpose. In another incident, reported by Shepard and Sanders, a captive bear was observed lying on its back and passing a chain back and forth from "hand" to "hand," apparently fascinated by the way the links fell over each other. Wildlife photographer Terry Domico once saw a brown bear "delicately turning a feather over and over in its paws" (*Bears of the World*, p. 6); he used the incident as an example of the bear's amazing dexterity with those clumsy-appearing claws, but it serves just as well to demonstrate the boundlessness of its curiosity. What animal other than a bear or a human would be interested enough in a feather to want to look at both sides of it over and over again?

Polar bears are often observed covering their black noses with their white paws in order to blend into the landscape better while stalking prey through the snow. This behavior does not show the uniformity one would expect from instinct: the bears that use it apparently either learn it from other bears or figure it out for themselves. In *Mammals of the Canadian Wild*, Adrian Forsyth tells of a polar bear that appeared to consciously

A young polar bear investigates a hole in the ice on a tundra pond.

imitate a chunk of floating ice while stalking a seal in the open sea. The bear had evidently deduced that seals can see better underwater than they can on the surface; it would go instantly limp each time the seal submerged, moving toward it only when it came up for air again. Eventually the seal surfaced right next to the bear, perhaps intending to climb out on the "ice." The bear grabbed it and bit its neck out.

Both polar bears and grizzlies have been seen deactivating traps by rolling rocks onto their trigger mechanisms, sometimes scouring an area several hundred feet in diameter to find a suitable rock. The animals are evidently well aware of the traces they leave behind. Grizzlies and blacks have both been known to evade human trackers by walking backward in their own tracks and by using rock outcrops and water to avoid leaving tracks altogether. Grizzlies almost always den up in the middle of a snowstorm, evidently so that the fresh snow will immediately conceal their tracks and keep the den from being found. In 1970, an experienced bear hunter named Harvey Cardinal was killed and eaten by a grizzly in the snows of northern British Columbia; the bear had apparently figured out that Cardinal was following its tracks, so it circled around a small hill and intersected its own path, allowing it to come up quietly on the intently tracking man from behind.

My favorite account of bear brain power, however, is the story of Blanche, a big, blond female grizzly trapped twice in the upper Flathead Valley of British Columbia by Canadian game biologist Bruce McClellan. As recounted by Terry Domico (*Bears of the World*, p. 59), the tale goes something like this: bear is caught in leghold snare, rubs ankle painfully raw by pulling snare tight around it while struggling to escape. Is shot in rump with tranquilizing dart and fitted with radio collar. Successfully evades recapture for three

A tundra buggy near Churchill, Manitoba, gets the once-over from a pair of intensely interested polar bears.

years. Is finally caught by leghold snare again; when discovered, is sitting quietly with the snare still comfortably loose around her wrist, her rump firmly planted in a shallow hole she has dug in the dirt to keep it out of the way of any darts that may come flying in that direction. Biologist darts her in the neck instead, receives extremely indignant look from bear as the animal collapses. You bastard, you're not playing fair. Give a gal a chance.

Intelligence like this does not evolve in a vacuum. Like all animals, bears are what they are because of what they do, rather than the other way around. Form follows function: an animal's characteristics are determined almost completely by the role it plays in its ecosystem. Niche is everything.

B E A R   N I C H E S

The concept of the *niche* is central to the science of ecology. The term refers to both an organism's home and to its job: that is, both to its physical place on the planet and to its functional place in the intricate web of relationships that keep the ecosystem it is a part of ticking smoothly along. There are thousands upon thousands of niches in each ecosystem, all of them subtly (or not so subtly) different from one another. Two organisms cannot occupy the same niche at the same time and place because the better-adapted of the two will always dominate the less well adapted one, either driving it to another niche *(competitive exclusion)* or eliminating it altogether *(extinction)*. The difference in adaptiveness does not have to be very great to be effective. Black bears are forest dwellers largely because grizzlies have competitively excluded them from open terrain, and in those places in the West where grizzlies have been exterminated a few blacks have begun to take that part of the niche back, colonizing what was formerly exclusively grizzly turf. Short-faced bears have been totally eliminated from North America largely because the Ursids—the blacks and grizzlies and polar bears—are marginally more successful at being bears.

In order to make sense of the extraordinarily complex and tangled web that makes up the niche system in even the simplest of environments, ecologists use a classification method that categorizes organisms by their *trophic levels*—their places in the food chain. At the bottom are the *producers,* the green plants and other organisms, such as algae and some bacteria, which can turn simple elements and sunlight into the complex organic compounds that are necessary for life. Above these are the *first-order consumers,* the organisms, primarily herbivorous animals, that eat the producers in order to obtain complex organics in a ready-made form. *Second-order consumers* eat the first-order consumers. At the apex of the chain are the *top carnivores,* which are big enough and fierce enough that nothing else eats them (although they may occasionally eat one another). As you go up the food chain, efficiency declines, so that a piece of land that supports 10,000 tons of producers may support less than a ton of top carnivores; this bottom-heavy phenomenon is known as the "pyramid of biomass," or sometimes—in honor of Charles Elton, the British biologist who was the first to thoroughly explore the concept—the "Eltonian pyramid." Tying the top of the pyramid to the bottom are the *decomposers,* the organisms, primarily bacteria and fungi, that break down the bodies of the dead and render them into elements again so that the producers can begin the cycle anew.

The problem with this tidy scheme is that it does not account for omnivores, which

do not so much fail to fit into the system as ignore it. Omnivores are opportunists, and will happily feed on any trophic level, as readers may discover for themselves if they put this book down to go feast upon a steak smothered in mushrooms with a glass of wine and a side order of salad. A bear would enjoy that meal every bit as much as you would, and would probably take it from you if it had the opportunity. Omnivores are the Magic Johnsons of the animal world: they can play every position on the court and make it look as though they belong there. Their niche—to mix sports metaphors a bit—is that of the pinch hitter. Whenever another animal falls down a bit on the job, or leaves its niche temporarily unfilled, the omnivore is there to take up the slack.

The key to this niche is flexibility, and the key to flexibility is intelligence. An omnivore must be able to recognize opportunities for food, even when they come in unfamiliar guises. It must be able to adapt its diet to what is available, meaning that it must be able to conceptualize the idea of substitution: if you can't catch the squirrel, you substitute the nuts in the squirrel's storehouse. It must be willing to experiment with new foods—and be able to carry out those experiments in ways that won't harm it (discovering that a plant is toxic is of very little value to an animal that dies in the process of making this discovery). And it must above all be able to learn easily, both from its own experiences and from the experiences of others of its kind. It must be able to build up a specific, individualized body of knowledge that is uniquely tailored to its own peculiar environment, the distinctive combination of biocenters and travel corridors that makes up what it has taken for its home range. Instinct cannot be tailored this way. Generalized knowledge can be passed on by the genes, but specific knowledge must be taught.

This intense need for learning colors everything about an omnivore, right down to

Demonstrating its species' omnivority, a black bear cub nibbles skunk cabbage (*Lysichitum americanum*) in the foothills of the Cascade Mountains, Washington State.

Bears eat meat when it is easily available, as when the salmon are running at Brooks River Falls, Alaska.

Pages 132–137:
In a face-off between two ecological niches, an omnivore (brown bear) confronts scavengers (western gulls, *Larus occidentalis*) over a McNeil River salmon. Bears almost always win these encounters, but many prefer to avoid argument by eating their catches in the water.

Humming contentedly, two brown bear cubs nurse from their watchful mother on the banks of the McNeil River. Mother bears usually lie on their backs to nurse their cubs.

the level of biological reproduction. Ecologists categorize all organisms into one of two distinct groups, depending upon their reproductive strategies. Most organisms are what are referred to as *r-selected*—they produce large amounts of young and count on the law of averages to make certain that some of them reach adulthood. The chances of any given r-selected infant reaching reproductive age may be extremely small, but if the numbers are large enough to begin with somebody is going to make it, and thus the gene pool can perpetuate itself. This is the strategy used by most plants and most prey animals. The legendary breeding rates of rabbits and guppies are perfect examples of the r-strategy in action.

The opposite of an r-selected species is known as a *K-selected species*. K-strategy organisms produce only a few young, but they protect and nurture them so that a large percentage of them reach adulthood. They are not content to allow the law of averages to perpetuate the species. They want to skew the odds a little bit in their favor. Uncontested first place in the K-selected derby belongs to humans. Second place depends on where you are. In Africa and tropical Asia, it is the great apes. In most of the rest of the world, it is the bears.

The K-selected life-style affects just about everything in a bear's life. It is responsible for the animal's curiosity, its excellent problem-solving ability, and its apparently near-photographic memory. It has led to the development of an impressive array of data-gathering machinery—the extraordinary sensory apparatus, the delicate manipulative ability—and of the cognitive skills and integrative capacity to put it all together. And it has dramatically affected the animal's life cycle, especially in terms of lifespan and child-rearing. Bears live a long time—thirty to forty years, even in the wild—because short lives would waste all that learning and the gene pool cannot afford the loss. And they reproduce extremely slowly because each generation must be taught as much as possible of what the previous generations have figured out, and that requires a lot more one-on-one, mother-and-child interaction than would ever be possible if the mother had to constantly be dealing with a brood the size of a rabbit's. Bears are not born knowing how to be bears. Each cub has to learn the art for itself.

BABY BEARS

Baby bears are born in the middle of the winter denning season, usually late January or early February. They are blind, naked, and almost totally helpless—so poorly developed, in fact, that for centuries there has been a persistent folk belief that they leave the womb as undifferentiated lumps of flesh, which are licked into shape by their mothers. Mother bears do nothing of the sort, of course, but they do wake up briefly during delivery, long enough to clean up the cubs and eat the afterbirth. Then they drop back into dormancy. The cubs remain awake. Their lessons have already begun.

The first order of business—crucial, because it is going to underlie all the others—is maternal bonding. In order to accept the sometimes harsh discipline that must be imposed on them as part of the teaching process, the cubs must have a strong emotional attachment to their mothers. This attachment is formed in the den, where the mother is the sole source of food and warmth, and the necessity of firmly establishing this essential bond is probably

Brown bear mother and three cubs-of-the-year, Naknek Lake, Alaska. Bears are strongly K-strategy animals: they produce only a few young, which they teach and care for intensively.

A pair of second-year brown bear cubs cuddle each other while they wait for their mother to return.

one of the reasons that the birth takes place when it does. The process works extremely well. A well-known behavioral characteristic of bear cubs is the "nursing hum," a low-pitched, throaty, contented humming like the sound of a purring cat or a very large bee, which cubs make while they are suckling. They will ordinarily only make this noise for their mothers. Dave Siddon of Wildlife Images, who has raised numerous orphan cubs, states flatly that he has never managed to earn the nursing hum from any of them, no matter how comfortable and bearlike he makes the nursing situation. (He has noticed, however, that pairs of cubs will make the nursing hum while they suck on each other's ears.)

Eventually the mother wakes up again, and the little family—it may consist of any-where from one to five cubs, although by far the most common number is two—emerges from the den, blinking a little in the sunlight. The time is usually late March, though it may be anywhere from late February to early May. The mother is not hungry yet, and will continue to live off her fat reserves for another week or more. The cubs are constantly hungry, but in between frequent bouts of nursing they will begin to explore the immediate environs of the den. The purpose of this brief interlude appears to be to give the cubs a carefully controlled introduction to the outside world. With her appetite depressed, the mother bear is able to keep her full attention on the cubs' behavior and make certain that their education proceeds. They must be walking well enough to keep up with her, and aware enough of the dangers caused by gravity, obstacles, and other animals to keep out of immediate trouble, before she can lead them away from the den and begin teaching them foraging and survival skills.

Socialization can be dangerous. This brown bear mother has herded her cubs up a hill beside the McNeil River and has turned to see if the large male that charged them is still pursuing them.

When the mother bear's "appestat" finally kicks into gear she leaves the den site, heading straight for the closest food source she knows about, the cubs plodding and tumbling along behind her. Now their education begins in earnest. All that spring and summer and into the fall they will trail their mother from biocenter to biocenter, learning which plants to eat and which to leave alone, and how much energy to put into chasing squirrels, and the dangers posed by wolves and humans and other bears. (Full-grown bears seldom need to fear wolves, but cubs do. Fear of wolves may be instinctive among polar bears. It is certainly deep-seated: polar bear cubs are so terrified even of small dogs that wild cubs will scamper toward humans for protection from them.) The young bears will learn how to construct daybeds to rest on during the heat of the afternoon, pulling together leaves and grass and small branches in a hollow beneath a bush or under an overhanging rock or—in the case of black bears—in the crotch of a large tree. They will learn how to bury windfalls of food, especially dead elk, cows, or other large carrion, by digging a shallow hole, dragging the carcass into it, and covering it with a thin layer of dirt and leaves and branches and sometimes small trees so that other animals will be properly forewarned: *this is a bear's cache; don't mess with it*. And they will also learn that with such food caches they will have to construct daybeds within easy watching distance, so that the cache can be protected against other bears that might happen along and decide to ignore the warning signs and dig it up for themselves.

The family will almost certainly den together for the cubs' first winter. The cubs will watch their mother locate a den site and dig a den, and will store away knowledge of how it is done. In the den they will curl up together, a vast furry ball of bear with three noses,

A remnant of snow provides a cool playground for a grizzly mother and her cubs on a hot day in Denali National Park, Alaska.

Opposite: A brown bear sow has decided to hold her ground as her cubs stand to watch a young boar pass within 100 feet. Mikfik Creek, Alaska.

Normally loners, bears
must practice good
social skills when they
gather in large numbers
at rich biocenters such as
the McNeil River Falls.

and all three will slide into dormancy, although the mother's sleep is likely to come sooner and go a little deeper than that of the cubs. (The cubs will also probably wake up sooner. Any human parent who has tried to sleep in Saturday morning can easily sympathize.)

In the spring of the cubs' second year the family once more emerges from the den together and the lessons begin anew. Most of them are repeats from last year, but there are variations. The cubs are older now, and able to take care of themselves better, and the mother is far more likely to make them do just that, abandoning them for up to two or three hours at a stretch. She is also more likely to bring them into close contact with other bears. Contrary to popular belief, bears are not totally solitary animals, but spend a fair amount of their lives in company with other bears. There are rules of bear society that the cubs must learn, and now—in their second year—is the time to teach them.

There are a variety of circumstances that will bring bears together, but the most common one is simply good eating. Bear ranges usually overlap each other, and at particularly rich biocenters the overlap may be extreme, with as many as forty or fifty bears using a single biocenter's resources on a regular basis. With this many animals involved, it will be rare for a single bear to ever have the biocenter all to itself; it is almost always going to have to share the area with others of its kind who have decided to visit the same restaurant at the same time.

And this means socializing. Constantly fighting with each other would be counterproductive: it would result in using up the energy the bears have gathered at the biocenter to obtain. When there is enough to go around, fighting over distribution is not only pointless but wasteful. Conservation requires tolerance. The bears must learn to get along.

Peaceful coexistence is attained in a variety of ways. Where the biocenter is spread out over enough ground—a meadowful of grass, a hillside of biscuitroot, a large garbage dump—the bears will spread out, too, leaving enough space between individuals that they do not have to directly interact with one another. When the food is concentrated, however, contact becomes inevitable, and the bears must be able to signal their intentions to each other to avoid fighting. Dominance hierarchies develop, with bears of equal rank tending to associate with each other and those on the lower rungs of the social ladder avoiding conflict with those higher up. The hierarchies are not genetically predetermined but are created and maintained empirically at each biocenter through the bears' previous experience with each other and through occasional tests of strength—rather like those found in any good-sized junior high school.

To maintain this rudimentary but well-defined social structure, the bears rely on an extensive vocabulary of gestures and vocalizations that meets most of the criteria of a language. Parts of this language are clearly instinctive: lowering the head to indicate submission, seeking eye contact to indicate aggression, flattening the ears against the skull to show anger, sitting down or moving away to show respect. Other parts are almost certainly learned. This is particularly true of vocalizations, which seem to be taught to infant bears the same way human language is taught—that is, by selective reinforcement. The cubs make a large variety of essentially meaningless sounds, which are eventually winnowed down to just those "words" that get the desired response from other bears. Some gestures may be learned this way as well, especially those involved with threat

Opposite: Even during the height of a salmon run, black bears, unlike brown bears, seem to prefer fishing solitarily. They often give up prime fishing holes when other black bears are present.

Juvenile brown bears
from two families greet
each other tentatively in
a meadow near Alaska's
Mikfik Creek.

Pages 150–153: Bear language: young polar bears test the social hierarchy at Churchill, Manitoba, Canada.

This mother at the edge of the McNeil River is displaying ignoring behavior toward the photographer, but her cub can't resist a peek.

At the McNeil River, a mother brown bear claps her paws together to warn another bear to stay away from her cubs. Bears may also slap the ground or a tree trunk as a warning gesture.

displays. A bear that is threatening to attack will usually—but not always—clap its front paws together or slap the ground with them, apparently to intimidate the enemy by making as much noise as possible. If a tree is available the bear may slap that instead, perhaps because it can make even more noise that way. "Gaping"—opening the jaws wide, as close as possible to the face of the other bear you are trying to impress—is probably learned by copying other bears, as is the technique known as the "bluff charge"—a full-tilt run at the other bear, pulling up short at the last moment. And learning is almost certainly involved in the development of "ignoring behavior," in which a bear faced with a possible confrontation does something else—or perhaps nothing at all—in a highly visible and ostentatious manner. This is the communication method of choice when a dominant animal wishes to indicate that it has no intention of enforcing its dominance if the other leaves it alone: "Just get the hell out of here, buddy, and we'll pretend I didn't even see you."

These and a full range of other "words" must be learned by the socializing cubs, and the rich biocenter setting is the place to do it. The mother bear will avoid the most common alternate bear social club, which is the mating ground. She is not in estrus, anyway, as long as she is nursing the cubs, and there is no sense exposing her children needlessly to the heightened aggression of male bears in heat. If a male does approach, she will chase him away. Among black bears, which are not sexually dimorphic, this is relatively easy. Among grizzlies and polar bears, where males may be two to three times the size of females, it is not as easy, but it still happens. A mother bear defending her cubs is such a potent force that not even another bear three times her size is likely to risk the fight.

A brown bear sow with her second-year cub relaxes in the warm afternoon sun. Mikfik Creek, Alaska.

A young brown bear
gapes to warn another
that it is too close.
Brooks River Falls,
Alaska.

Bear mothers abandon their offspring toward the end of the cubs' second summer. The process is often emotionally stressful for the young bears, as this recently abandoned Denali National Park grizzly juvenile is discovering.

When adolescent brown bears are cast off by their mother, they often seem lost. Occasionally, they'll wander curiously close to humans, investigating campsites. This behavior has earned them the title "hooligan." Mikfik Creek tidal estuary, Alaska.

Pages 160–165:
Siblings of bear species
often live and travel
together for several years
after their mothers have
abandoned them.

Tagging, radio
telemetry, and long-term
studies will, with luck,
reveal more about bear
relationships.

The family may den together for its second winter as well as its first, but this will not necessarily happen, and even if it does the cubs will surely be sent off on their own before the next year's breeding season. They will probably stay together for some time after their mother abandons them, traveling and feeding side by side and denning together for two or three more years. Sometimes these sibling friendships last well into adulthood. Dave Siddon likes to tell the story of the logging crew near Coos Bay, Oregon, that telephoned him one spring day a few years ago: they had unwittingly dropped a tree right onto an occupied bear den, and a mother bear had erupted from it and run away, abandoning her cubs. Could Wildlife Images take care of them? Siddon agreed to do this, and the logging crew brought the two orphaned infants to him. A week later they were back with two more: another felled tree had flushed another mother bear, denned up only fifty yards or so from the first. "The four cubs were almost identical," Siddon says. "You had to figure the mothers were a pair of sisters who had denned up next to each other."

Pages 166–167: A young black bear in the dense forest near Wrangle, Alaska. Bears almost always avoid humans if they are given the choice.

Siblings are not the only bears who form lasting friendships, by the way. Apparently unrelated bears will sometimes team up, traveling, foraging, and playing together for weeks or even years. Very little is known about these relationships other than that they exist. When the partners are two females with cubs there are some obvious advantages in terms of baby-sitting availability and mutual defense, but when the friends are both adult males—a pattern that is seen fairly commonly among polar bears—nothing seems to be clear beyond the fact that the bears obviously like each other. Clearly the whole subject of bears as antagonistic loners needs a close critical look.

6 A
PLACE
FOR
BEARS

Some years ago I spent a summer weekend backpacking through the Siskiyou Mountains with a stockbroker from Medford, Oregon, named Bryan Frink. Our route took us through Sucker Gap, a large flat saddle containing several small rocky knolls and grassy meadows, interspersed with forest and backed on the south side by a tall cliff of dark, glossy metamorphic rock. We entered the gap from the north, winding down the Boundary Trail from Swan Mountain. It was midmorning on a bright, sunny day.

I was perhaps fifteen paces in the lead as we came to the crest of the southernmost knoll in the saddle. There was a tall cedar at the edge of the last of the meadows, thirty feet or less in front of me, and beneath the cedar was a resting bear. No, not a resting bear: an explosion of bear, a blur of bear, plummeting south toward the alder thicket at the base of the cliff 100 yards away. There was a series of crashing thuds as the bear disappeared among the alders. Bryan came up beside me.

"Wow," I said.

"What was that," he asked, "a rockfall?" The three or four seconds it had taken him to catch up to me was all the bear had needed to disappear totally. Bryan had heard the crashing, but he had not seen so much as a single hair.

This is the closest encounter most of us will ever manage to have with a truly wild bear—a streak across the meadow, a great shaggy rump disappearing into the alders, the sound of something heavy breaking things up in the center of the thicket. One suspects, given the bear's bloodthirsty reputation, that this is the way most of us would prefer it. *Keep them critters away from me 'fore I get et. Let me look at 'em in a zoo, with a good strong set of bars between us. Or give me a nice .30-06 with telescopic sights.* A perfectly understandable position, to be sure. But is it fair—either to us or to the bear? Do we really need every square inch of our shared niche strictly for ourselves? Should there not be a place for bears —a place where they can go on being bears, without being converted either to prisoners or to rugs? Or—even worse—to roadside panhandlers?

I personally believe that such a place is not only desirable but necessary. I believe that anyone who cares about the future of humanity must also be concerned about the future of bears. The pioneering grizzly researcher John Craighead has said it best. "If the human species cannot preserve the grizzly bear, it probably cannot preserve itself," he wrote in 1982, "for the type of human behavior that will permit extinction of the grizzly will also permit the extinction of mankind." To ensure our own future it is first necessary to ensure a future for bears. Craighead is almost certainly right.

It does not necessarily follow, however, that the task is going to be particularly easy.

A bear that has learned to beg food from humans is one crucial step removed from the wild and may no longer be able to survive on its own. *Opposite:* In Manitoba, Canada; *page 171:* along the Alaska Highway, Alaska.

Habitat loss is the biggest single threat to all the world's bear species. Clear-cut, Olympic National Forest, Washington.

I have the following from an unimpeachable source, which must, for obvious reasons, remain nameless. The scene is a contemporary bear hunt somewhere in northern California. A group of hunters have released their dogs, and the dogs have treed a black bear. One of the hunters takes careful aim and shoots—not to kill the bear but to shatter its spine, paralyzing its hind legs, so that it will fall out of the tree and the dogs can rip it apart alive. The dying bear struggles among the dogs while the men laugh. Then suddenly it is not quite so funny: the bear has managed to grab one of the dogs in its jaws. The dog yelps. The dog's owner pulls out a knife, walks over, and casually stabs the already mortally wounded bear in the eye.

All this is not only observed but videotaped, for the entertainment of those present and the edification and elucidation of their young.

I know, I know: bears do it, too. There are well-documented accounts of humans being attacked and killed by all three North American species of bears, and many of these attacks have been as senseless and unprovoked as the so-called hunting incident I have just described. But there is this to be said for the bears: they have not come anywhere near driving their competitors out of the niche and off the continent. We have. Niche competition is an extremely formidable force. Gause's Principle has killed more bears than all the hounders who have ever lived can ever even think about.

When Europeans first brought firearms and farming to North America in the early seventeenth century, grizzlies ranged from the Pacific eastward into what is now Minnesota, northward to the Arctic tundra, and south into Mexico. No reliable estimate of their

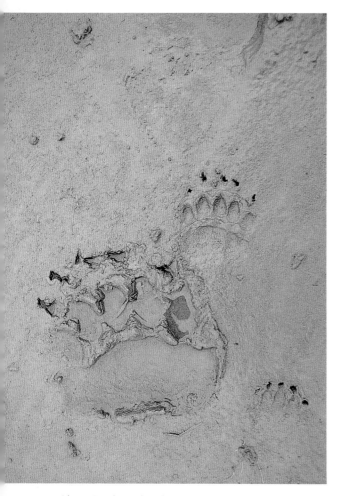

Above: Fresh tracks of a mother brown bear and her cub call for extra caution from human travelers along the banks of Alaska's Mikfik Creek.

Right: This brown bear path has been worn deep into hard tundra on Kodiak Island by generations of bears that have not only followed the same route but stepped in the same footprints. Locating human trails and campsites away from traditional bear travel corridors is an effective means of preventing bear attacks.

numbers exists, but it was probably in excess of 500,000. Today, between 50,000 and 90,000 remain. Roughly 20,000 of these are in Alaska; nearly all of the rest roam the Yukon and the Canadian Rockies. Less than 1,000 inhabit the forty-eight contiguous states of the continental U.S.: 650 or so in Montana, perhaps 200 in Wyoming, and a scattered one or two dozen in the far northern parts of Washington and Idaho, scrunched up against the Canadian border. In California, where grizzlies—the so-called golden bears —were once so numerous that they fed in herds and are still featured on the state flag, the last recorded individual was shot in 1922. (A remnant few were rumored to be hanging on into the seventies in the nearly impenetrable fastness of the state's northern mountains.) In Colorado, extinction apparently took place around 1950: a single individual was killed by a bowhunter in the southeastern corner of the state in 1979, but a thorough search failed to turn up any others, and it is thought that this particular bear was either the absolute last of its kind or an errant beast from Wyoming with a bad case of wanderlust. The last grizz was killed in Texas in 1890, in New Mexico in 1931, in Oregon in 1933. Even the relative health of the populations in Montana and Wyoming may be an illusion: despite decades of concentrated research, it is still not certain whether either state's grizzly numbers are actually high enough to be self-sustaining.

The black bear is doing better. Estimates of its current North American population range from 300,000 to 750,000, which is probably in the same neighborhood that it has been for at least four centuries. Black bears are found in at least twenty-three of the fifty states: New York has 4,100; Pennsylvania has 7,500; and even urbanized New Jersey— the most densely populated state in the Union—has between 60 and 100. Thirty thousand

The most dangerous bear is one that has been startled by a human's approach.

If we successfully preserve the black bear, how careful must we be to preserve its various subspecies? *Above:* Kermode bear, British Columbia Coast Range; *opposite:* glacier bear, Glacier Bay, Alaska; *overleaf:* cinnamon bear, Sierra Nevada, California.

blacks roam the woods of my home state of Oregon; about the same number can be found in Washington and in Maine. The overall numbers for the species may even be increasing; certainly the animals are moving into marginal areas, such as northern Quebec and the high Rockies, where they have not historically existed.

Before we get too sanguine about the situation, however, we also need to look at the pressures on their population—pressures that have increased dramatically in the last decade or two. This is recent enough that it may be too early to tell what the effects will ultimately be. Bear hunting as a form of "entertainment," for example, appears to have substantially increased; it has certainly become more efficient, as unsportsmanlike bear "hounders" are now using radio-tracking devices to home in on study bears wearing radio collars. (Some wildlife rehabilitation clinics have stopped trying to track their bears after release because of the danger posed to the animals; the average length of time between release of a study animal and its death at the hands of hounders has shrunk, in some areas, to as little as three months.) A related hazard is posed by the growing illegal traffic in black bear parts, especially gallbladders (used in Chinese folk medicine) and paws (an expensive delicacy in restaurants throughout the Orient). With the Asian black bears nearly wiped out, the principal source of these materials has shifted to North America, and so far it is running far short of the demand. For the poacher willing to risk the penalties, the rewards can be great: bear-paw soup retails for as much as $800 a bowl, and single bear gallbladders have sold at open auction for as high as $55,000 (black-market prices typically run even higher). The poaching problem is large enough that, in order to begin to get a handle on it,

California was forced to close its bear-hunting season entirely in 1990—the first time in the history of the Golden State that such a closure had taken place.

In 1952, 3,000 American black bears were slaughtered to provide fresh busbies for the honor troops involved in the coronation of Queen Elizabeth II. Is this an appropriate end for such an intelligent animal? If there were a sudden series of rapid turnovers in the British monarchy, would the bear be able to survive?

The greatest threat to the future of black bears, however—insensitive pageant designers and overenthusiastic hunters aside—is the same as it is for grizzlies: habitat loss. These are woods-loving animals, and their woods are disappearing around them. The principal villain here is probably not forest practices such as clear-cutting, which if properly handled does not harm the bears and may actually benefit them by providing extra forest-edge habitat. The greatest incursions into black bear habitat come not from lumberjacks but from suburbanites. Cities are sprawling farther and farther into their surrounding woods; vacation-home developments are proliferating in once-pristine high-mountain regions. This may be the real reason that we are seeing black bears in northern Quebec and other places that they did not formerly occupy. It may be that they are spreading into these fringe areas not because they like them, but because they may no longer have anyplace else to go.

Polar bear numbers are extremely difficult to estimate, and very little is positively known about them. It is thought that there are approximately 15,000 of the big white bears worldwide, and the data seem to indicate that this number has remained relatively stable for the last several hundred years. But here again there are some disturbing trends.

According to experts on bear behavior, if a bear charges, your best tactic is to stand your ground and shout in the hope that it is only bluffing, as most are. Avoid eye contact with the animal. Alaska Range, Alaska.

Increasing resource exploration and development in the far north brings humanity farther and farther into this most remote of bear habitats. Tourism—often with the bears themselves as the attraction—has also increased dramatically. One discomforting result of this increased pressure is being noted in Alaska, where female polar bears which have traditionally built maternity dens on land are now denning far out on the sea ice. It is too early to tell what this behavioral change bodes for polar bear reproductive success.

No, let me broaden that statement. It is too early to tell what effects any of the rapidly accelerating trends of the last ten years are going to have on the populations of any of these bears. These are, remember, the ultimate K-selected North American species. They have long lives and extremely low reproductive rates. The impacts of population trends begun in the 1980s are not likely to be noticeable until after the year 2000, and by then it may be too late to reverse them. Will bears go with us into the new millennium? Or will we finally have the niche all to ourselves—only to discover, too late, that we really had come to enjoy the company?

One thing is certain: we are not going to preserve our niche mates without an effort. Because we do share a niche with them, conflict is inevitable. Managing that conflict is the only way to reduce it to tolerable levels for both species.

Much research has gone into this problem over the past several decades. Most of it has been directed at reducing the harm caused by individual "problem" bears—that is, those that have injured humans or their possessions, or have shown by their behavior that

The polar bears around the southern end of Hudson Bay constitute a clearly distinct population with a far more southerly distribution than others of their species. Is this unique population worth preserving if to do so will interfere with proposed hydroelectric developments in the James Bay watershed?

At Katmai National
Park, Alaska, bears and
people have learned to
interact with a minimum
of interspecies friction.

Opposite: As the number of humans watching her continues to increase, how long will this Mikfik Creek brown bear mother continue to tolerate them?

they have a high probability of doing so. A lot of things have been tried, with varying degrees of no success, and we still do not know what really works.

The traditional method of dealing with a problem bear has always been to shoot it, and this is still sometimes done; but as wildlife biologist Monte Barker of Idaho's Shoshone National Forest has pointed out—tongue firmly in cheek—killing problem bears is "a bad way to deal with a threatened species." (Barker himself advocates the use of specially trained dogs to keep bears away from humans; he is particularly high on the possibilities of a Russian breed known as the Karelian bear dog, which is said to be "utterly fearless" around bears.)

Another firmly entrenched traditional approach is relocation: trapping the problem animal and trucking or helicoptering it to some remote site from which it cannot find its way back to the area where it was causing trouble. The difficulty with this approach is that it does not factor in the bear's intelligence, determination, and pathfinding ability. It is next to impossible to relocate a bear so that it cannot find its way home. Black bears in Michigan and grizzlies in Alaska and Montana have been tracked as they made their way back to familiar territory from release sites more than 150 miles away; polar bears have homed over twice that distance. Nor does it seem to do any good to place barriers in their way. One Alaska "nuisance" grizzly that was transported to a remote island in Prince William Sound turned up four weeks later back at the site it had originally been captured, having swum at least nine miles of open ocean and covered more than fifty miles on foot in the interim. Lynn Rogers, who has studied the phenomenon among black bears in Minnesota, believes that bears are able to home primarily because of their incredibly sensitive sense of smell; they sniff the air in various directions until they detect a familiar odor borne by the wind, and then literally "follow their noses" home. Others have suggested that the animals somehow have developed the ability to detect the earth's magnetic field. Whatever the cause, the rate of recidivism among relocated problem bears is so high

Relocation of problem bears, like this airlift of a nuisance polar bear at Churchill, is useful only as a short-term holding action.

Opposite: Hands on its knees, a contemplative brown bear relaxes in a meadow at Pack Creek, Admiralty Island, Alaska.

as to render the technique largely useless; it is, as Stephen Herrero has aptly put it, "usually not much more than a holding action."

Aversive conditioning is a relatively new technique that shows some promise, but it too is probably ultimately doomed to failure. In this technique, captured nuisance bears are placed in a holding pen and subjected to unpleasant surprises of various types—loud noises, electric shocks, having their rumps peppered with rubber bullets—any time they approach a human or a human approaches them. They are left alone at all other times. Eventually they learn to associate the presence of humans with unpleasant experiences and start avoiding human contact, at which point they can safely be graduated back to the wild. Or so the theory goes. Charles Jonkel of the University of Montana is probably the leading exponent of aversive conditioning, which he has practiced on more than sixty bears, both black and grizzlies, in a facility near Missoula; of these, he states that only two have caused further trouble after they have been released. He cites this as evidence that the technique works. Others are not so sure. "Bears are not sight-oriented, they're scent-oriented," points out Dave Siddon once more, somewhat wearily. "And even when they're being aversive conditioned, they're still being fed on food that's been handled by humans and picked up human scents, so they're still going to associate people smells with food. Aversive conditioning doesn't create bears that are afraid of humans—it just creates bears that are afraid of humans who are banging pots and pans and carrying cattle prods." And Siddon's doubts appear to be borne out by management experiments in Great Smoky Mountains National Park, where for a while panhandling bears were chased away from the roadsides by park personnel every time they were encountered. The hope was that the bears would learn to avoid humans altogether, but it was a vain hope. "What the bears quickly learned," writes Stephen Herrero, "was that tourists gave handouts and rangers harassed them."

In the end, we may have considerably more luck managing ourselves. We are, after all, supposed to be the more intelligent species. Learning is our specialty. If we and bears must learn to avoid each other in order for the bears to survive, shouldn't we be doing most of the learning to avoid?

To prevent destructive contact between bears and humans it is often most successful to manage the humans.

PROTECTING OURSELVES FROM BEARS

Actually, learning is not even required for much to be accomplished in the way of human management: there are many potential improvements that turn out to be passive, in the sense that no behavioral change is necessary on the part of the people who are being managed. For example, humans tend to follow trails and camp in established campsites, even in the backcountry; to minimize bear encounters, it is necessary only to locate these trails and campsites so that they stay out of bear biocenters and travel corridors, such as willow bottoms, horsetail swamps, and south-facing meadows. Campsites can also be enclosed in bearproof fences—a technique that has been tried successfully in Glacier National Park. Hikers can be outfitted with "bear bells"—small bells attached to clothing and

Pages 186–189:
Grabbing some rays, a
polar bear basks in the
weak northern-latitude
sun at Churchill. Polar
bear fur is a highly
efficient solar collector
built on fiber-optics
principles. Note the
furry soles of the paws.

Opposite: A pair of second-year cubs wait for their mother in the shallows of Alaska's McNeil River.

packframes which ring as their wearer walks, alerting any bears in the vicinity that there is a human coming (bears will generally avoid human contact if they have enough advance warning; it is usually only surprised bears that are dangerous bears).

Other techniques are active, in the sense that they require the humans involved to make a conscious effort to change their behavior, but even these are usually not particularly difficult to carry out. Trails can be posted with warning signs, or even closures, when bears are known to be using an area. Campers can keep food and garbage in sealed containers to minimize temptation. Cooking creates savory odors that attract bears—sometimes from several miles away—and linger in clothing and hair; it is therefore probably best, in areas known to have problem bears, to avoid cooked foods altogether. At the very least, clothing should be changed following the cooking and eating of the meal, and these activities should take place well away from the sleeping area. Foods of all sorts should be kept out of tents. Women should probably avoid hiking in grizzly country while they are menstruating, as there is strong circumstantial evidence that the odor of menstrual blood is a powerful bear attractant. Sex isn't a particularly good idea, either. It appears to have been the odors of sexual intercourse that attracted the bear that killed and ate a pair of teenage employees of Lake McDonald Lodge in Glacier National Park in July 1980.

When charged by a bear, the natural tendency is to run away. The word from all bear experts is, Don't. Running from a bear will trigger its prey-pursuit behavior—and it can run at least twice as fast as you can. Climbing a tree may be useful in grizzly country—if you can find a tree tall enough to get you out of the reach of the bear—but this technique is of little or no use around black bears, which are excellent climbers (a skill they probably evolved to get away from grizzlies themselves). The best technique is simply to stand your ground and hope that the bear is engaged in a bluff charge, which most of them are. Avoid meeting the bear's eyes; it will see that as an aggressive move on your part. Shouting and waving your arms, however, are usually a good idea.

P R O T E C T I N G   B E A R S   F R O M   H U M A N S

All these are techniques that can be used to protect humans from bears. What about the reverse? How do we change human behavior to protect bears from humans?

This is a much knottier problem, and one that does not appear at all easy to solve. Its scope is different. Humans tend to be endangered by individual bears. Bears are endangered by individual humans, too, but their greatest threat comes from the whole of humanity. We want the niche totally to ourselves; we want their place in the world as well as our own. And in most places we have got it. What little scraps we have left for the bears may not turn out to be adequate. A human can avoid bears by going to New York City, or Seattle, or Kansas, or any place else the bears aren't. Where can a bear go, today, to avoid humans?

In Montana and Wyoming together there are someplace around 800 to 900 grizzlies, in two populations—one centered in and around Yellowstone National Park (about one-fourth of the total) and the other centered in and around Glacier National Park. In the two parks the bears are protected, and humans may be carefully managed to avoid conflict

Clearly in its element,
a young polar bear
rests amid ice floes in
Hudson Bay.

with them. Unfortunately, the parks are nowhere near big enough to support a self-sustaining population of grizzlies. In order for Yellowstone to have grizzlies, the Absaroka–Beartooth Wilderness must have grizzlies, and the Cooke City–Miles City region must have grizzlies, and some of the surrounding foothills and grasslands must have grizzlies, too. In order for Glacier to have grizzlies, grizzly rights must be preserved on a large area of adjacent lands to the south and west—the Bob Marshall, and the Cabinets, and the Kootenais, and various points around and beyond and in between. It is on these extra, nonpark lands where the real conflicts occur. Few people would seriously suggest that bears should be eradicated from the national parks, but there is a large contingent of those who feel that they should be eliminated everywhere else. What they still somehow fail to grasp is that to kill the bear everywhere else is also to kill it in the parks.

How much room does a bear need? When is a population endangered and when is it not? Do we have an obligation to make the world safe for them bloodthirsty critters, anyhow? Whose obligation is it?

This is not something on which everybody can easily see eye to eye.

The grizzly has been on the threatened species list in the forty-eight contiguous states since shortly after the list was first drawn up, back in the early 1970s. For the last five years there has been a spirited effort in Montana to delist it. Some Montana residents—including a fair number of biologists—argue that the 650 bears estimated to inhabit the greater Glacier National Park region (known as the northern Continental Divide population) are sufficient to declare the species no longer threatened, and that it should now be managed like any other game animal. Others see the move as a thinly veiled plot on the part of the state to wrest control of grizzly management from the federal government, which maintains its authority only so long as the bear continues to be listed under the Endangered Species Act. They believe that the state's count of the animals is not accurate enough, and that it may not be sufficient to preserve the species anyway, and that not enough attention has been paid to the effects of recent invasions of grizzly habitat by clear-cuts and mining, especially in the Cabinet Range of western Montana. The argument has boiled over in the newspapers, with one reporter comparing the grizzly-management beat to covering civil-rights activities in the South in the 1960s. Meanwhile, with no clear direction, management of the bear flounders. A limited hunting season has been in effect since inception of the threatened-species listing in 1975: hunters are allowed to kill bears until reported bear deaths from all causes exceed twenty-five. In most years, only a small fraction of those twenty-five deaths are attributable to hunters. In one recent year, thirty-three grizzlies were shot in Montana. Six of these were killed by hunters; the rest were either done in by poachers or killed by animal-control officials as "problem" bears. Can the bear population continue to sustain this mortality rate? Is it evidence that the population is in good shape, or is it contributing to the population's decline? The questions do not seem to be currently answerable.

And—ignoring the grizzlies for the moment—what about the black bears? Overall, their numbers appear to be holding steady or even increasing. Do we need to be concerned about them? The answer becomes considerably more complicated when you remember that at one time what we know as the single species *Ursus americanus* was subdivided into more than eighty geographically separate "species." We now consider these to be merely separate populations, color phases, races, or at most subspecies. How many of these do we

need to preserve? If the black bear as a whole is doing well, do we need to preserve the kermode bear or the glacier bear? What about the Louisiana black bear, and the Texas black bear, and the Olympic black bear, all of which Merriam considered separate species but which do not have the visual flash of the white kermodes or the blue glacier bears? Do all these varieties of bears need to be preserved? If so, how? If not, why? Which ones? Where? Where do you draw the lines, and what gives us the right to draw them anyhow?

For most of these questions there are no right answers. There are only choices—and in wildlife management, as in many other fields, choices often have a way of being made before we understand what it is we are choosing between.

Katmai National Park, in Alaska, has the best bear-management record in the United States. The big grizzlies fishing the Brooks River are one of the prime attractions of the park, and the bears must constantly deal with a press of watching tourists; despite this, there has not been a bear "incident" at Katmai since 1966, and that one wasn't fatal. Katmai does it by managing humans, not bears. Bears have the right of way under all circumstances: photographers and fishermen are not allowed to approach closer than fifty yards. Campers are required to cook in a central area away from their tents, and to store all food in bearproof caches provided by the Park Service. Fishermen cannot clean their catches on the streambank, but must take them to a secure "cleaning shed" where the offal may be disposed of in a manner that does not attract bears. These regulations are drilled into the heads of visitors in an orientation lecture that all are required to attend. Violators risk expulsion from the park.

Surrounded by gulls, an old boar brown bear sprawls wearily on the McNeil's bank.

We are cautioned
against reading our own
emotions into the
expression of other
animals, but who is to
say this polar bear is *not*
smiling at the falling
snow? Churchill,
Manitoba, Canada.

Opposite: Brown bear and rainbow, Pack Creek, Admiralty Island, Alaska.

Yet Katmai, too, may be in trouble. It is in real danger of stumbling over its own success: its reputation as a place where one may safely watch grizzlies has spread, and its visitor load has increased asymptotically, from 11,000 annually in 1981 to 50,000 a year today—a fivefold increase in ten years. There is every indication that this trend will continue. At what point are the tourists going to overwhelm the bears? When does someone get hurt, or killed, despite the strictest precautions? When do the numbers of people reach the point that the bears, weary of dealing with them, quietly fade away? Park officials are wrestling with these questions now. They are not optimistic. Both bears and visitors are necessary to the existence of the park, but dealing with the conflicting needs of the two groups is becoming an increasingly acrobatic juggling act, and no one is certain just how much longer all the balls can be kept in the air.

Ultimately, the question is going to arise, at Katmai as well as at Glacier and Yellowstone and New Jersey and Pennsylvania, Why preserve the bears at all? The standard fallback position of environmentalists—that we need to keep all the niches in the ecosystem filled for the sake of stability—doesn't work here, because the bear's niche is the same as ours. The environment does not need bears. They are big, and dangerous, and in direct conflict with us for food and living space. Why do we insist on keeping them around?

And here, at last, is a question we can answer. We keep bears around because, although the environment may not need them, the human spirit does. We need them because the mountains are too empty without them, the wilderness too tame, the nights too secure. Because without the bears to compete with we will no longer have any real excuse for being human.

At southern Oregon's Wildlife Images rehabilitation center, Dave Siddon muses on this point. "Everyone says what a wonderful service we provide for wildlife," he says, hunched over a chair in his small, crowded office. "But we're not providing a service for wildlife—we're providing a service for people who *care* about wildlife. We provide a human service for people who care enough to bring animals to us. We think they need to be encouraged to continue to care.

"I have been asked by reporters how I can justify spending $8,000 on a baby bear when children are starving. My answer has always been to point out that we as humans are the only organisms capable of caring for other animals. It's the main thing that makes us human. If you can't spend $8,000 on a baby bear, why bother to spend hundreds of thousands keeping a human alive? The fact is, if we look on *Homo sapiens* as the only life form worth saving, it probably isn't." Outside the door of Dave's office an orphaned grizzly cub, found huddling near its train-killed mother by railroad workers in Montana, pads through its pen like a small furry tank, while in the next pen a half-grown American black bear, rescued from a pet store in Rome by a group of Italian animal-rights activists, lies on its back, points all four of its extraordinarily humanlike feet skyward, and tries in vain to walk on the round orange ball of the sun.

A polar bear prowls the
coast of Hudson Bay
near Churchill,
Manitoba, Canada.

Bibliography

Anthony, H. E. *Field Book of North American Mammals*. New York: G. P. Putnam's Sons, 1928.

"Bad News Bear." *Discover* (Dec. 1987): 8.

Bruemmer, Fred. "Diary of a Bear Watcher." *International Wildlife* (Sept./Oct. 1989): 46–51.

Burt, William Henry, and Grossenheider, Richard Philip. *A Field Guide to the Mammals*. Boston: Houghton Mifflin Company, 1964.

Craighead, John J.; Sumner, J. S.; and Scaggs, G. B. *A Definitive System for Analysis of Grizzly Bear Habitat and Other Wilderness Resources (Wildlife-Wildlands Institute Monograph No. 1)*. Missoula, Montana: University of Montana Foundation, 1982.

Domico, Terry, and Newman, Mark. *Bears of the World*. New York: Facts on File, 1988.

Forsyth, Adrian. *Mammals of the Canadian Wild*. Camden East, Ontario, Canada: Camden House Publishing, Ltd., 1985.

Gittleman, John L., ed. *Carnivore Behavior, Ecology, and Evolution*. Ithaca, New York: Cornell University Press, 1989.

"Grizzly Encounters Pose Challenge to Western Parks." *National Parks* (Jan./Feb. 1988): 14.

Grossmann, John, and Alt, Gary L. "Learning to Live with Bears." *National Wildlife* (Apr./May 1990): 4–10.

Herrero, Stephen. *Bear Attacks: Their Causes and Avoidance*. New York: Nick Lyons Books, 1985.

Laycock, George. "Making Bad Bears into Good Bears Could Spare Bears." *Audubon* (Mar. 1987): 22–28.

McNamee, Thomas. *The Grizzly Bear*. New York: Alfred A. Knopf, 1984.

Mills, Judy. "End of the Line for French Bears?" *International Wildlife* (Jan./Feb. 1989): 5–10.

Mirsky, Steven D. "Solar Polar Bears: Polar Bear Fur Sets a Standard for Solar-Energy Converters." *Scientific American* (Mar. 1988): 24–26.

Pond, Caroline. "Bearing Up in the Arctic." *New Scientist* (Feb. 4, 1989): 40–46.

Revkin, Andrew C. "Sleeping Beauties." *Discover* (Apr. 1989): 62–65.

Robbins, Jim. "When Species Collide." *National Wildlife* (Feb./Mar. 1988): 21–27.

Rogers, Lynn. "Home, Sweet-Smelling Home." *Natural History* (Sept. 1989): 61–67.

Rue, Leonard Lee, III. *Pictorial Guide to the Mammals of North America*. New York: Thomas Y. Crowell Company, 1967.

"The Russians Are Coming." *Discover* (Mar. 1990): 16.

Savage, R. J. G., and Long, M. R. *Mammal Evolution: An Illustrated Guide*. New York: Facts on File, 1986.

Schemnitz, Sanford, ed. *Wildlife Management Techniques Manual*. Washington, D.C.: The Wildlife Society, 1980.

Schullery, Paul. "Yellowstone Grizzlies: The New Breed." *National Parks* (Nov./Dec. 1989): 25–29.

Shepard, Paul, and Sanders, Barry. *The Sacred Paw: The Bear in Nature, Myth, and Literature*. New York: Viking Penguin, Inc., 1985.

"Why Polar Bears May Follow the Sunspots." *Science News* (May 19, 1990): 318.

"Your Letter Can Help Save the Grizzly Bear!" (pamphlet). San Francisco: Sierra Club, Nov. 1990.

Opposite: Dry autumn grass forms a playground for a lone polar bear cub on the tundra near Churchill, Manitoba.

Index

Opposite: Grizzly bear, Denali National Park, Alaska.

Habitat preservation is
the only way to ensure
the survival of all bear
species.